"Robbie is a brilliant event design strategist, and a calm, confident Zoom technician. He is creative and sharp, quick-thinking, and always focused on results. Engage with Robbie before outlining an event, because I can assure you that whatever you have in mind is not quite as impactful as what Robbie can help you create.

I enthusiastically hired Robbie because our event guests deserved the kind of seamless experience that only happens if the 'stars on stage' aren't fumbling around trying to pull the strings as event producers and directors."

—KATE COLBERT, marketer; speaker; researcher; communications expert; and author of the bestselling books *Commencement: The Beginning of a New Era in Higher Education* and *Think Like a Marketer: How a Shift in Mindset Can Change Everything for Your Business*

"As a small non-profit organization, Robbie has truly transformed our virtual meeting experience for everyone. His professionalism and expertise not only alleviated a burden on staff, but his unique ability to care for and support speakers and attendees resulted in better, more interactive sessions. Since Fall 2020, he has become a trusted member of our team and community!"

—LENA WORKMAN, California WIC Association

"Thank you for hosting the National Speakers Association (NSA) Mic Swap. You run the most efficient and effective of all the networking Zoom meetings I join each month. Your question prompts are great for getting people to connect in the breakout rooms in a real way. You provide a great space of inclusivity, and you do a phenomenal job of shining the light on certain people that makes them feel special while also helping us learn from them. It's a masterclass on how to run effective Zoom networking events."

—JEFF HARRY, Positive Psychology Play Speaker; Top 100 HR Influencer

"We engaged Robbie as the producer for our first-ever virtual conference in Fall 2020. Robbie was key to its success. He provided operational support and project management and understood what needed to happen to avoid problems and keep everything running smoothly. He went beyond our expectations of event planning and being a producer of the event. He was great."

—ROSS TARTELL, Ph.D., Association of Talent Development (ATD), Southern Connecticut Chapter

"We could not have pulled off our virtual events had we not had Robbie on our team! He helped us with more than the day itself. He conducted a speakers' training to help them pivot their in-person style to fit the virtual presentation, which takes minor changes but yields great engagement results. He also took our schedule and built a 'run of show' so we knew what would happen every minute and who was up next. We also utilized Robbie's emcee skills as he helped us navigate the day and stay on time. He added great DJ skills, too."

—LAURA BIEWER, Notary Symposium

"I highly recommend Robbie for his services as a Zoom consultant and facilitator. He supported my team for a virtual Feeding America conference over the past couple of years. I really appreciate how present and enthusiastic Robbie is in all of our interactions, as well as his wealth of knowledge on how to make virtual meetings inclusive and engaging."

—MEGAN WHITNEY, Feeding America

"Robbie has been the one to help us take our Zoom game to the next level. We were doing it, and it was fine, but it was more mechanical and transactional. Since he came into our mix in early 2022, he's added the relational part. That warmth is coming through. We can only do that through the skill of an excellent producer. I want to honor him for being that. He's the best!"

—MELANNIE DENISE CUNNINGHAM, Creator
and Executive Producer, The People's Gathering: A
Revolution of Consciousness Conference; Greater
Tacoma Peace Prize recipient

"I used all Robbie's tips and tricks at our board meeting the day after he led a Zoom training, and they were a big hit. We used one of his prompts in the breakout rooms and kept the energy up with music and ASL applause. Everybody loved it! If you have a high-stakes meeting that needs excellent facilitation and engagement, reach out to Robbie for expert assistance."

—MARGI POWER, Leadership Council,
San Mateo County

"I enrolled in The 5% Advantage Program—because I thought I should know something about Zoom in these tough times. When the program was over, I was amazed to find new doors opening. Because of Robbie's training, I've learned useful skills to take my business in a new, exciting direction. The day I received my Certified Virtual Event Professional #NoMoreBadZoom digital badge, I got two bookings for my new program. After 35 years in the speaking and broadcasting business, being able to jumpstart a brand-new business at the age of 86 is a gift beyond price. If you have the opportunity to take this program, do it."

—DOROTHY WILHELM, author; speaker; broadcaster;
and newspaper columnist

"Robbie is a brilliant Zoom trainer. I joined his free #NoMoreBadZoom Virtual Happy Hour in 2020 and enjoyed the tips, tricks, and strategies he shared. When I saw that he was offering The 5% Advantage Program to make us 5% better every time we Zoom, I thought, 'I don't need that. I'm already a seasoned speaker, and I teach other people how to lead events.' But there was something about the program promise that called to me.

I'm so glad I answered that call. Robbie's program filled in the blanks I didn't even know were there. The program has tremendous depth, and while I already had two virtual presenter certifications, the one I got from Robbie's course was the most intensive and helpful to my success in leading virtual programs. Continuously learning is essential, as tech is ever-evolving. I highly recommend him and his program."

— MARILYN SUTTLE, keynote speaker; author, *Who's Your Gladys? How to Turn Even the Most Difficult Customer Into Your Biggest Fan*

BREAK OUT
OF BOREDOM

BREAK OUT
OF BOREDOM

Low-Tech Solutions for
Highly Engaging
Zoom Events

ROBBIE SAMUELS

Wordsworth Lane Press
Philadelphia, PA

Edited by Linda Popky
Interior design and composition by Jeanne Schreiber
Cover design by Adam Renvoize

Print ISBN: 979-8-9877950-0-2

ebook ISBN: 979-8-9877950-1-9

Printed in the United States of America.

10 9 8 7 6 5 4 3 2 1

LIBRARY OF CONGRESS CATALOGING-IN-PUBLICATION DATA

Names: Samuels, Robbie, author.

Title: Break out of boredom : low-tech solutions for highly engaging Zoom events / Robbie Samuels/

Description: First edition. | Philadelphia, PA : Wordsworth Lane Press, [2023] | Includes bibliographical references.

Identifiers: ISBN: 979-8-9877950-0-2 (paperback) | 979-8-9877950-1-9 (ebook)

Subjects: LCSH: Zoom (Electronic resource)--Handbooks, manuals, etc. | Videoconferencing-- Handbooks, manuals, etc. | Internet videoconferencing--Handbooks, manuals, etc. | Event planners--Handbooks, manuals, etc. | Business meetings--Management. | Special events-- Management. | Meetings--Planning--Management. | Communication-- Technological innovations--Social aspects. | Interpersonal communication--Technological innovations-- Social aspects. | Group facilitation--Technological innovations--Social aspects. | Telecom- munication--Social aspects. | LCGFT: Handbooks and manuals. | Instructional and educational works. | Self-help publications. BISAC: BUSINESS & ECONOMICS / Business Communication / Meetings & Presentations. | BUSINESS & ECONOMICS / Entrepreneurship.

Classification: LCC: HF5734.7 .S26 2023 | DDC: 658.4/5602854678--dc23

Download Free
Bonus Resources

READ THIS FIRST

To help you implement the strategies in this book, I've created several resources, including checklists, step-by-step guides, and 30+ videos. Download them all at no cost whatsoever. It's my gift to you.
– Robbie Samuels

Go to www.robbiesamuels.com/breakout to get it!

This book is dedicated to the participants who
showed up on March 13, 2020, for my
first virtual happy hour.

I had just come to accept that after ten years of
growing a speaking business, no one needed to learn
about networking AT conferences, or engaging and
welcoming in-person event design.

Their enthusiastic response to my virtual facilitation
skills helped me realize I could apply my expertise
and skills in new ways during these challenging
times. I no longer felt irrelevant.

Without their encouragement, none of this
would have happened.

Table of Contents

Preface

How do you write a book about a technology that changes constantly? That was my challenge at the start of this project more than a year ago. I decided to focus on purpose-first design and virtual facilitation principles applicable to any platform, even if the buttons are in a different place.

If you find the steps in this book don't match what's on your screen, the links in the *Endnotes* will direct you to the latest update for that feature. The specific steps may change—some did as I was writing this book—but the "why" is a constant.

My hope is that as you read this book, you'll be inspired to look beyond the limitations of Zoom and focus instead on the possibilities afforded by virtual events. I hope that you will strive to become 5% better every time you Zoom.

This book is a culmination of what I've learned as a virtual event design consultant and executive Zoom producer, supporting organizations over the last three years. I wrote this book to share these learnings with my fellow speakers and facilitators so that we can collectively elevate the Zoom experience for our participants.

I've always believed that events are about content AND connection. Since the pandemic disrupted in-person events, virtual events are no longer an exception. They can (and should) be transformative, inclusive, and engaging.

I also wrote this book for my fellow conveners, the event organizers and meeting professionals who don't know what they don't know as they commit to creating remarkable virtual events. This book will help you select the right team to support you. I'd be honored to be a part of that team.

Introduction

Do you remember what you were doing on March 13, 2020, when a worldwide pandemic brought all in-person events to a screeching halt?

Some of us jumped into learning Zoom to stay relevant as a speaker or educator. That's the day I hosted my first virtual happy hour, not knowing where it would lead. Other folks hung back, hoping this would not be a big disruption and that life would return to "normal" within a few weeks or maybe a few months.

Regardless of which camp you fell into in 2020, it's likely that you now have Zoom basics down. The problem is that basic skills are not enough to stand out as a top-notch virtual presenter. Your message may not be getting across if you're not providing a thoughtful structure that allows *everyone* to engage.

All too often, traditional event design, particularly in a virtual setting, benefits the loudest, most confident, and most experienced participants.

How can we structure our events so that everyone feels welcomed instead of merely invited? That's the mission of this book.

The Zoom virtual event platform you're using today is not the one you were using in 2020. So much has changed. I wrote this book to help you get up-to-speed with the latest features and facilitation techniques.

> *But this is so much more than a technical guide. As you read this book, you'll begin to see how Zoom can create transformative, inclusive, and engaging online experiences.*

This book is not just about Zoom
While I'll be focusing on how to leverage Zoom, the online facilitation and event design concepts I cover will apply to any platform.

I didn't set out to be an authority on virtual event design strategy and Zoom production. Like you, my pre-pandemic plans were rerouted. Before the pandemic, I spent over a decade working to be recognized as a networking expert—specifically networking at conferences and helping organizations create more intentionally inclusive and welcoming events.

During that time, I . . .

- Presented my signature talk, *Art of the Schmooze,* for over ten years.[1]

- Launched a podcast, *On the Schmooze,* about leadership and networking.[2]

- Published my first book, *Croissants vs. Bagels: Strategic, Effective, and Inclusive Networking at Conferences.*[3]

- Presented a TEDx talk, *Hate networking? Stop bageling and be the croissant!*[4]

- Published my first *Harvard Business Review* article, "Why Business School is a Great Time to Network."[5]

I was poised to be an overnight success—ten years in the making.

And then, March 2020 hit. Suddenly, anything in person just . . . didn't exist anymore. No one needed any of the skills or expertise for which I had become known. Everything I'd worked on for ten years was irrelevant. All that momentum I'd built for a decade was just . . . gone.

My mantra became *Show up and add value.*

This mantra led to me hosting my first virtual happy hour on Friday, March 13, 2020. It was on a whim, but I knew my network was going to need ways to stay connected. That one-time event became the weekly #NoMoreBadZoom Virtual Happy Hour, which I'm still hosting, as of this writing, three years later.[6]

FIGURE 0.1. Quickly I became sought after for my Zoom knowledge. In May 2020, I launched *The 5% Advantage Program*, a program to help speakers and meeting professionals become more confident and

competent using Zoom.[7] By the third month it became a certification program and dozens of students became Certified Virtual Event Professionals #NoMoreBadZoom, helping them pivot or relaunch their careers.

By the fall of 2020, several organizations were seeking out my support to help them bring their events online with less stress and greater participant engagement. I swiftly reinvented myself as a virtual event design consultant and executive Zoom producer.

By the end of 2020, I had a thriving six-figure business based on all new revenue streams. I wrote my second book, *Small List, Big Results: Launch a Successful Offer No Matter the Size of Your Email List,* to answer the question I kept hearing, "Robbie, how did you grow a thriving six-figure business so quickly? In a pandemic, no less!"[8]

In this, my third book, I'm sharing the lessons I've learned producing, hosting, and speaking at hundreds of virtual events since March 2020. I am writing this book because I believe events are about content AND connection, and virtual events are NOT an exception. We need to learn how to reimagine virtual events—not recreate or replicate what we did in person. If we focus on achieving specific outcomes for our participants and create intentional engagement, we'll hit a home run every time.

Unfortunately, many virtual presenters have not evolved their skills beyond the basics they learned in 2020. This is what's causing Zoom fatigue. No matter how enticing the content, participants will be turned off by poorly designed sessions and sloppy online facilitation.

Bob Bejan, corporate vice president of global events, production studios, and marketing community at Microsoft, stated in a May 2020 *Fast Company* article,

"Whereas in-person events are more theatrical in nature, virtual events require a cinematic approach. Many experienced presenters are theatrical—we've trained ourselves to project and fill the room with our presence when we're on stage.

But now, we need to retrain ourselves to fill the computer screen. There is no crowd, so we need to tone it down and tune in. We need to learn to have an engaging conversation with our audience directly via the camera."[9]

I know for certain now what I could have only hoped to see in mid-2020—that virtual presenters can create a transformative, inclusive, and engaging experience, and we don't need all the bells and whistles to do it.

I'd love to hear what resonates with you in this book and how you were inspired to take action. Email action@BreakOutofBoredom.com to share what you discovered was possible, or if you have any questions.

My team and I would love to lower the stress for you and your team by providing virtual event design strategy and Zoom production support. Details are available at www.robbiesamuels.com/virtual-event-design.

CHAPTER ONE

Reimagine the Possibilities

"Never doubt that a small group of thoughtful, committed citizens can change the world; indeed, it's the only thing that ever has."

–Margaret Mead

Since the pandemic required us to rethink how we bring together our communities and share information, I have had the pleasure of working with outstanding organizations focused on important missions, such as eliminating food insecurity, providing nutrition and wellness for new parents and babies, and building anti-racist communities.

Rather than finding technology limiting or interfering with communication and connection, I've helped my clients create dynamic, engaging, and intimate virtual conversations with hundreds of participants during an event. Here's an example from my work on The People's Gathering: A Revolution of Consciousness Conference, a convening hosted by Pacific Lutheran University-Graduate Programs and Continuing Education twice a year.

Borrowing from their website description, this convening is a professional and personal development learning experience that provides a supportive space where participants can engage in frank and open dialogue about race and racial disparities systemically present in work, school, and everyday life. Local and national social justice scholars and activists from Indigenous, African American/Black, Asian, Latino, Multiracial, Pacific Islander, and white communities lead small group discussions to increase participants' intercultural competence.[1]

The conference design was very intentional before I joined the team. Over 500 participants logged into Zoom for a full-day conference. The convening opened with five minutes of silence, while a slide show explicitly acknowledged the presence of Native American, Alaska Native, and Indigenous people and their continued struggle for justice, followed by the names of the hundreds of Black and Brown men and women killed by police officers across America, the rise in Asian American and Pacific Islander hate crimes, and Indigenous women gone missing. The host offered a welcome and overview and reiterated that the training is designed to unapologetically "decenter" whiteness and teach from an anti-racist lens.

The morning session included a keynote speaker who invited participants to stay engaged through chat prompts. In the second half of the day, participants selected a different Zoom room to join, based on how they responded to the U.S. Census questions around race and ethnicity.

Based on previous convenings, we knew that the room with white participants would likely have about 300 participants. The plan was to assign the 300 people randomly to a 30-minute breakout room facilitator-led discussion about the morning program's keynote. With that in mind, I trained 30 volunteer facilitators on how to hold space for deep conversations on Zoom. Before the event, I was asked by the lead facilitator whether participants could self-select one of six topics for a second breakout room discussion. Topics included race + higher education, race + incarceration, and race + healthcare.

We still needed to set up groups of about 10 participants per breakout room, so inviting participants to self-select a topic through the **Let Participants Choose Room** feature would not have worked. I needed to figure out an easy way to weave this into the existing program timeline. After examining a few options, we made a decision. At the start of the afternoon program, participants were asked to add a three-letter code to the front of their name to indicate which topic they would like to discuss during the second breakout room.

While the facilitator led a debrief in the main room following the first breakout room discussion, I used these three-letter codes to manually assign each participant to one of the 30 rooms by topic, keeping the number of participants to about 10 per room. This allowed participants to have deep and meaningful conversations around their specific topic and race. These race dialogues were intimate, facilitated, and led to the client's desired outcome—participants committed to taking specific action to become more anti-racist. When asked about this design strategy after the event, my client said, "You brought expertise that helped us fine-tune our execution."

Creating this same experience at an in-person event would have taken a lot of coordination and a large conference space that could hold more than 50 tables with 10 or 12 seats per table. Pre-assignments would be required, and last-minute assignments would be challenging. The onus would be on participants to be in the right place at the right time. Late arrivals would cause disruption.

> *In March 2020, I could not have envisioned designing this kind of experience on Zoom. Now, I believe Zoom made the experience smoother and resulted in more people participating.*

Since 2020, I've been producing multi-day virtual conferences for the California WIC Association. Even after in-person events became possible again in 2022, they decided to continue providing virtual programming. Their reasons?

- More equitable and inclusive of all staff—especially front-line staff

- Provides greater access to national experts

- Concurrent live sessions are recorded, so the entire agenda is available for learning

- Recordings are available long after the live virtual event, which has led to more participants earning continuing education (CE) units[2]

Through strategic design and speaker training, we are hosting virtual events that are engaging and fun, with opportunities for participants to connect—without the stress of putting on a multi-day in-person conference.

When the pandemic began and virtual events became a daily, if not hourly, occurrence, many organizations reacted by shifting their programs online. The problem was that the model they were familiar with for virtual programs was 45 minutes of death-by-PowerPoint followed by ineffectual Q&A and no one moderating chat—a typical webinar.

It became apparent rather quickly that people attended events for a mix of content AND connection. Virtual could no longer be talking heads hiding behind slides and ignoring participants. Virtual events needed to provide a mix of content AND connection.

Another issue was that many organizations tried to replicate their in-person event. That didn't always translate and limited all the new possibilities offered through virtual that were not available in person.

> *No one considered how restrictive in-person events had been.*

I've attended in-person conferences held over three days with 12, 20, or even 42 concurrent sessions. I've attended conferences that took over the entire downtown of a major city, with more than a mile between sessions. That happened because in-person events require people to be, well, in person. Therefore, the event is restricted to as few days as possible to reduce the cost for the organization and participants. If the plan is to take what had happened in person and move the same schedule online, it would be replicating a restriction, not an asset of in-person events.

Instead, a virtual event could be spread over days, weeks, or even months. This creates more opportunities for community-building and learning, and increases the likelihood that participants will stay connected to the organization.

As in-person events became possible again in 2022 and 2023, many have assumed hybrid is the goal. If by hybrid, you mean an event that simultaneously supports an in-person and virtual audience, I'm not a fan. To do this correctly requires an out-sized budget to cover technology, staffing, and intricate strategies—and could still leave one or both audiences feeling dissatisfied with the experience. Instead, my goal is to share ways to increase engagement during virtual events, which could be scheduled before or after an in-person event—or in place of an in-person event.

> *Instead of replicating in-person events, reimagine them.*

PURPOSE-FIRST DESIGN

Before deciding the format, it's essential to begin with the end in mind, a.k.a. purpose-first design. Since you can't achieve everything all at once in a virtual event, you must be very clear about your objectives.[3]

QUESTIONS TO ASK YOURSELF AND DISCUSS WITH YOUR TEAM:

- What is the purpose of this event? What are we trying to achieve? More importantly, what's the promise our participants hope we will keep?

- What is the outcome our participants have identified as the measure of a successful event?

- What will the transformation be by the end of the session? Transformation meaning that participants will go from feeling/ thinking/doing one thing to feeling/thinking/doing another:

FROM	TO
Feeling _____________	Feeling _____________
Thinking _____________	Thinking _____________
Doing _____________	Doing _____________

For example, participants will go from feeling apathetic to excited. They'll go from asking why rock the boat to thinking it's time for a change! They'll go from living with the status quo to taking action to implement change.

Having this in mind and agreed upon by your team will help you select the right tools, exercises, and flow for your session. Every time you wonder whether to include a tool/exercise, come back to the question of purpose-first design. Would that particular tool/exercise help your participants have this transformation?

While there are many possible choices of objectives, it often comes down to just two from the perspective of your participants. They attend events hoping to learn relevant new information and make awesome connections. If you design your event with that top of mind, regardless of the other objectives you've identified, your event will be a success from the participants' perspective.

Design the event in segments

Have a clear understanding of how each segment (topic/ exercise/breakout room) impacts a particular objective. This way, if you need to shorten your presentation, you'll know which segment to skip. Over time, you may end up with 10 or more segments and be able to mix and match them depending on the time allotted and the objectives for that particular event. In this way, you'll be ready for a 45-minute session, a 90-minute session, or even a three-hour session.

WEBINAR VS. MEETING: WHAT'S THE DIFFERENCE?

Before you dive into the rest of this book, let's clarify the differences between Zoom meetings and Zoom webinar platforms.

These two Zoom products are very similar in their design, but one big difference is that when you are presenting in a Zoom meeting, you can see the participants (and they can see each other). In contrast, participants in a Zoom webinar are called attendees because they don't have cameras and they're not actually participating. They're *attending*.[4]

When designing your virtual event, the event's purpose should help you decide whether Zoom meeting or Zoom webinar is the better choice. By default, the max participants per Zoom meeting is 100, but with a **Large Meeting add-on**, up to 1,000 participants can join the meeting. The max number of attendees for Zoom webinars ranges from 500 to 5,000, depending on the license you purchase. Log-in at www.zoom.us/pricing to upgrade to a **Large Meeting** or Zoom webinar.

One of the benefits of using Zoom meetings is the ability to use breakout rooms. (As of this writing, Zoom webinars don't offer breakout rooms, but Zoom may release this feature in 2023.) Even if breakout rooms aren't part of your event, a Zoom meeting may still be the best choice, as it allows the speaker to see participants while presenting. Even while sharing their slides, a speaker can set up their screen to view up to 24 participants. Being an energetic and engaging presenter is challenging when you can't see any participants. It feels like you're presenting to a brick wall. That's enough of a reason in my book, literally, to choose Zoom meetings if you have fewer than 1,000 participants.

My bias is based on my experience. Generally, webinar presentations are a lot less engaging, with the speaker staying behind their slides and not interacting very much with the attendees. Some speakers have learned to overcome this by having fewer slides and asking for comments in chat throughout their talk.

Another consideration is that each Zoom webinar speaker must be assigned a unique link to join the webinar. I mention this because getting this unique link to each panelist requires a bit of extra attention to detail that you won't have to think about at all with a Zoom meeting.

There is an option to enable a **Practice Session** so you can get comfortable with the platform before starting the webinar. Use the **Practice Session** to meet with panelists and run through a Green Room Checklist before starting the webinar. Unlike a Zoom meeting waiting room, you cannot message attendees waiting for the webinar to begin nor see who is waiting.

Sample Green Room Checklist
Download this checklist and other resources at
www.robbiesamuels.com/breakout.

Meetings and webinars comparison[5]

Feature	Meeting	Webinar
Participant roles	• Host and co-host • Participant	• Host and co-host • Panelist • Attendee
Audio sharing	• All participants can mute/unmute their own audio • Host can mute/request to unmute participants • The host can set all participants to mute upon entry	• Only the host and panelists can mute/unmute their own audio • Attendees join in listen-only mode* • The host can unmute one or more attendees
Video sharing	All participants	Host and panelists
Screen sharing	✓	✓
Capacity	Up to 100 with free license; up to 1,000 depending on plan and large meeting add-on	Ranging between 500-5,000 attendees, depending on the license
Participant list	Visible to all participants	Visible to host and panelist
Email reminders	N/A	If registration is enabled
Chat	✓	✓
File transfer	✓	✓
Whiteboard	✓	✓
Annotation	✓	✓

Feature	Meeting	Webinar
Polling	✓	✓
Surveys	✓	✓
Livestream	✓	✓
Registration	✓	✓
Closed Captioning	✓	✓
Recording	✓	✓
Breakout rooms	✓	N/A
Practice session	N/A	✓
Waiting room	✓	N/A
PayPal integration	N/A	✓
Require password to join	✓	✓
International dial-in numbers	✓	✓

*__Note__: If the host or co-host enables **Allow to talk** for an attendee, that attendee can enable their microphone as well as mute and unmute themselves.*[6]

DON'T CALL IT A WEBINAR!

Be honest. If you sign up for a "webinar" that turns out to be a Zoom meeting—do you keep your camera off and engage in multitasking? You're not alone.

> *When we hear the term "webinar," we have a very clear set of expectations–none involving being on camera and participating. Language matters when it comes to your online events—and so does setting the context.*

If you're meeting using Zoom meetings, not Zoom webinars, then participants can see each other and be seen by the presenter. You can design the session to include breakout rooms for small group discussions. But none of that matters if nearly all participants join the call with their cameras off and plan to be in listen-only mode while walking the dog or doing the dishes.

It's not their fault, though, if the invitation said it was a webinar. They were not told to be camera-ready and prepared to actively engage. If most participants have their cameras off, the speaker won't see reactions to their presentation. When this happens to me, I feel like I'm presenting to a wall and hoping it's going well. I've been known to pause before starting my remarks or introducing the first speaker to say, "If you want an engaged presenter, it helps to have an engaged audience. If you're willing to turn on your camera, that would be greatly appreciated." Saying this has always resulted in most participants turning on their cameras.

Just like sharing the dress code in an invitation for an in-person event, it helps to share expectations for your virtual event invitations. Bottom line: If you hope participants keep their cameras on and actively participate, don't call it a webinar!

MAKING THE CASE FOR LIVE VS. REPLAY

I've had a few clients ask me to set up their virtual event as a Zoom webinar, not a Zoom meeting, because they don't want participants to see how few people showed up.

Here's the thing—if this is the reason you're choosing to use Zoom webinar instead of Zoom meeting, you're solving the wrong problem. Instead of worrying about how few people decided to attend the live presentation, make a stronger case for attending live, versus waiting for the replay video to be released. If you've been hosting lackluster Zoom sessions for the last few years, you've trained participants to skip the live session and plan to watch the replay instead. Unfortunately, the likelihood that even a majority of people who are given access to the replay will watch it is very, very slim.

Yes, there are reasons to record virtual programs and share the replay. I'm not against that idea. I believe that attending live versus watching the replay should be a qualitatively different experience. If it's not, then that's why you have so few people making an effort to attend the live session.

Here are a few ways you can increase engagement during the live session:

- Add a networking breakout room segment at the beginning or end of the program.

- At the beginning, this could be just a quick six-minute breakout room with three participants per room who share a recent win.

- At the end, you can randomly assign four to five participants together into breakout rooms for 10 to 15 minutes so they can discuss what they just learned.

- During an all-day or multi-day event, add a 10- or 15-minute breakout room segment after every session and before a 10 or 15 minute break.

- Train speakers to weave polls, interactive chat, and breakout rooms into their sessions.

- Assign someone to be the chat moderator, so easy questions can be answered in chat.

- Empower the chat moderator to interject if the speaker should answer a question during the presentation instead of waiting until the end.

- Reserve at least 15 minutes for Q&A throughout or at the end of the presentation.

Why is it better for people to attend live versus wait for the replay?

If you can't answer that question, then whether to choose Zoom webinar vs. Zoom meeting is not the issue. It's that you're not making the case for why people should attend live. And instead, you're paying extra money to hide the fact that not many people are attending your event.

There are many benefits to having an intimate gathering of fewer than 20 people, 50 people, or 100 people—whatever number you think is small. If only a few people attend but have a fantastic experience, that might lead to more people wanting to come live. If you can make the case, you may change the paradigm. If you've trained your audience to expect to be off-camera because you've been using Zoom webinar—it's time to reset expectations. You'll need to let them know to be camera-ready, and in a quiet space where they can unmute so they can fully participate.

Take a group photo of their smiling faces to post and ask participants to share their experience of your newly designed, intentionally welcoming, and engaging virtual event.

WORKING WITH A ZOOM PRODUCER

Juggling all the technical aspects of Zoom while presenting—the waiting room, chat, polls, and breakout rooms—can feel like trying to land a jumbo jet, having only read part of the instruction guide. Whether you hire a professional Zoom producer to manage all the tech or train an assistant to manage chat, get support if you have more than 20 participants. Don't try to do it all by yourself.

What is a Zoom producer, and why would you want to hire one? In April 2020, I began hearing about the concept of a Zoom producer from fellow members of the National Speakers Association.[7] The idea was to find someone with Zoom experience who could, for example, set up breakout rooms.

I soon realized that while many people could technically handle the breakout room setup, few could provide strategic guidance on how to leverage the breakout room experience.

TECHNIQUE, NOT TECH

In September 2020, a large healthcare organization reached out about an employee engagement event they needed to shift to Zoom. I was asked some questions via email before we had an opportunity to meet over Zoom. Here is part of our conversation illustrating the difference between hiring someone to push buttons and hiring a virtual event design strategist.

Their question:

Can we do two different sets of breakout groups during the course of the event? And, can we have more groups (each with fewer people) during the second set? (To clarify: people would be in a 10-minute breakout group with a group of 10 people, then be moved to a 10-minute breakout group of five people?)

My reply:

Yes. Easily. You can randomly send participants to the first breakout room and recreate the room to randomize the room assignments (changing the number of participants per room). However, there are best practices for how many participants for X minutes in a breakout room. I don't recommend 10 participants in a breakout room for 10 minutes.

My response opened a dialogue, and the person with whom I was corresponding wanted to know more about the timing and my reasoning. This created an opportunity to share more about how I could support their organization as a virtual event design consultant and strategist, as well as a Zoom producer.

I shared with them:

I evaluate my client's plans, reconfirm their objectives, and guide them toward leveraging digital tools and online facilitation to achieve that outcome.

I've developed best practices around the following:

- How to frame the breakout session question—to prevent the first person from getting a "hot seat" or therapy session, decreasing the likelihood that everyone else gets to share.

- How to set up the question/prompt instructions—so it's more likely to be discussed in the breakout session.

- How to help participants quickly determine who goes first in the breakout sessions and who goes next—to get the conversation started quickly and keep it going.

- Creating a breakout room debrief plan that involves every participant with highlights from just a few people—so the debrief is contained to five minutes or less.

- How to arrange the debrief so the best answers/stories are shared with the entire group—with a focus on hearing from diverse voices.

- The amount of time minimum to have per person is dependent on the objective of the breakout session:

  - General introductions: Three people for six minutes.

  - Discussion: Four or five people for 10 minutes (with a thoughtful prompt/question is critical).

  - Workshop exercise: Up to six people without a facilitator for up to 15 minutes; or, more than six people with a facilitator (and optionally a scribe) for more than 15 minutes.

I don't know for sure, but it seemed like the Zoom producer with whom they had been working on other virtual events simply answered "Yes" to all their questions without providing any guidance around virtual event design strategy.

I was quickly hired, and that contract pushed my revenue over six figures for a business that had only been conceived earlier that year. It was this client who first began calling me an executive Zoom producer, which I've found helpful as a way to distinguish my level of expertise.

> *The first six months, from March to September 2020, was a huge learning curve for me and required a lot of experimenting. It's wild to look back to this email exchange and realize that I stand by all of these best practices two and a half years later. You'll be learning more about each of them throughout this book.*

You may decide to hire a virtual emcee separate from your producer, or your producer may handle both roles. Either way, make it clear who should unmute to intervene when something is amiss. If a speaker forgets to unmute, you only want one person unmuting to point that out. Same thing if they aren't correctly sharing their slides, or the video they're sharing has no sound. Decide ahead of time who will keep the meeting humming when there's a glitch—whether pointing out a technical issue, or handling the introduction when the speaker who was supposed to do it loses their internet connection.

I speak from experience about this. My clients will attest that one of the main reasons I'm invited to support their virtual events throughout the year is my ability to remain calm in chaos, handle tech curve balls, and step in as an emcee whenever needed.

I was producing an event when the speaker private messaged me via chat to let me know her internet was spotty. She confirmed that I knew the plan for the next breakout rooms, just in case. While we were debriefing the breakout room activity, mid-sentence, she disappeared. I counted to three, unmuted and finished her sentence to the best of my ability. I then asked the next person who had their hand raised to share their thoughts. We were close to the end of the meeting, and I was considering ending five minutes early, but I kept an eye on the participant list to see if the speaker had rejoined. Two minutes passed before the speaker was back. She unmuted to apologize and take back the microphone. I received several private and public messages in chat, acknowledging how smoothly I had handled the situation.

This was in May 2020, when we were all still getting our bearings. What I did then stood out, but this is now a requirement for anyone promoting themselves as a Zoom producer or virtual emcee.

Another time, the person who was supposed to introduce the main speaker disappeared just as I was about to spotlight her. Fortunately, this organization took my advice and provided me with a script for each introduction. I unmuted, and explained that so-and-so is having some technical difficulties, but it would be my pleasure to introduce our next guest. I then proceeded to make the introduction, using the text the organization had provided. Her internet was working again by the end of the presentation so she could manage Q&A, but I was ready to fill in if needed, because we had a clear plan before the event began.

When I meet with a new prospect, there's sometimes pushback around how much structure we will create within the event. There's a common misconception that magic will happen by merely bringing people together. That's not true for in-person events, and it's definitely not the case for virtual events.

Magic happens when participants feel more comfortable because they understand the rules for engagement. This will lead to them participating more fully. Have you experienced being thrown into a breakout room without clear instructions? Participants stare at each other for a moment because everyone is muted, and it's unclear who should go first. It wasn't clear what you should be discussing, and you notice there's no countdown clock, so you have no idea how long you'll be in this limbo state.

It's not comfortable—especially if you're shy, introverted, younger, older, a person of color, and/or it's your first time meeting these people.

Inevitably, someone does unmute, and you're regaled with their stories until the 60 second countdown pops up, so you can hit the escape button to be brought back to the main room. The difference between this experience and one where everyone feels welcomed into the conversation is structure and quality online facilitation. That's what you're going to learn in this book.

Here are other ways that an experienced Zoom producer can help you create a fantastic event:

- **Speaker Strategy:** Meet with presenters to help them create the strategy for their session using purpose-first design.

- **Speaker Prep:** Meet with all presenters to share best practices for presenting virtually.

- **Green Room:** Meet with all presenters 30 minutes before the event start to run through a checklist that includes checking A/V and screen sharing.

- **Chat Moderator Prep:** Train team members to manage chat and track questions.

- **Debrief Meeting:** Lead a discussion post-event.

In this book, I'll share what you need to know so you can train a team member or someone in your community to support your virtual presentations. But keep in mind that working with an experienced Zoom producer will elevate your event, lower your team's stress, and increase retention. It's a worthwhile investment.

Zoom producer or chat moderator?

There is not a nationally or internationally agreed upon training or certification for someone to call themselves a Zoom producer, so it's important to know what kind of support you need and check references before hiring someone for this role.

A chat moderator would not need to be knowledgeable about the technical aspects of Zoom. Their job is to monitor the chat and keep track of questions or replies to chat prompts from the speaker.

CHAPTER TWO

Getting Set Up for Success

Imagine being invited to speak at an in-person conference. You took care to prep your slides, practice your speech, and even purchase a new outfit. You feel ready. A moment after you take the stage, you realize that you had forgotten to confirm with the host that you had slides, and now there's no projector booked for this room! That would never happen, right?

Well, for presenters using Zoom, that happened a lot in 2020. This happened to me as a participant in a session focused on showing us various Zoom features. When the facilitator went to set up Breakout Rooms, it became clear that the Breakout Room feature was not enabled in that Zoom account. We were instructed to leave the meeting and sign back in so the updated setting could take effect. As we did so, I heard the facilitator say, "Last time this happened, we needed to wait 30 seconds before coming back in."

The last time this happened??

If this happened once, there should be a process to ensure it never happens again. That's when I created my first #NoMoreBadZoom Settings

Checklist.[1] This is similar to the A/V rider professional speakers use to list their A/V needs (e.g., lavalier microphone, flipchart, special seating arrangement). Virtual presenters use this checklist to communicate to an organization what Zoom settings need to be enabled or disabled.

In this book, I'll refer to Zoom features you may not have enabled in your Zoom account. My students in The 5% Advantage Program are working to become Certified Virtual Event Professionals #NoMoreBadZoom. I tell them that before making a recipe their own, they must have the basics of a recipe to riff off—including all the required ingredients and necessary equipment. That means you might want to skip to *Settings* in Chapter Nine to ensure you have all these settings enabled so you can mix and match these features to create a fabulous event.

Chapter Nine covers the following:

- Account, Profile, and Desktop Client Settings

- Recording Options & Settings

- Update Zoom

- Meeting Settings

- Setting Up Polls, Surveys, and Live Streaming

Feeling confident your Zoom settings are up to date?
Keep reading this chapter. If you cannot access a feature I describe, you'll be directed to the *Settings* chapter to enable it.

Are you interested in becoming a Certified Virtual Event Professional #NoMoreBadZoom? Join the waitlist for The 5% Advantage Program at www.the5percentadvantage.com. The goal is to get 5% better every time you host or speak online—consistent improvement.

FIGURE 2.1. Certified Virtual Event Professional #NoMoreBadZoom badge.

YOUR AUDIO & VIDEO

In this section, I'll cover six key areas related to your A/V setup:

- Eye Contact

- Lighting

- Video Framing

- Virtual Background Dos & Don'ts

- Camera

- Audio

Eye Contact

What's the easiest way to convey to someone that you're speaking to them? Look at them. Unfortunately, when speakers and facilitators look at participants' videos instead of their camera, the opposite happens—there's a disconnect.

One time, I was producing an event around a sensitive topic, and the facilitator was casually leaning on her elbow with her face close to the screen while she selected who would speak next. She murmured empathetically while each participant shared her story. All the while, we were staring at the facilitator's forehead, because she was staring down at the participants' videos and not the camera.

Looking at the camera as often as possible while presenting is a simple step toward creating a connection with participants. Should you stare at the camera the entire time? No. It's ok to look away while you're thinking, to glance around at the gallery to see how participants are receiving your message or to read your notes—but look back at the camera as you make your point. This is important even when you share your screen because you're still visible.

FIGURES 2.2. and 2.3. A demonstration of how looking AT the camera creates a connection with participants.

Over the years, I've heard several great tips for how to train our eyes to look at the camera:

- Put a piece of tape right above your camera.

- Tape a photo behind your camera (so it's peeking over the edge of your laptop or desktop) or cut a hole in the photo to tape it over the camera.

- Use those "Sign Here" sticky arrows to direct your eyes toward the camera.

- My favorite comes from Elisabeth Steele, a fellow Zoom expert who teaches lawyers how to Zoom in style: Stick googly eyes above your camera so you can make "eye contact"—Hah![2]

To help you keep your eyes on the camera, it's important to figure out where to put all the Zoom windows (videos, chat, participant list), your notes, and any other windows or documents you'll be sharing or referring to during the meeting. Getting these windows open and arranged on your screen in an optimal layout may take trial and error.

Here are some tips:

If you don't have slides but do have notes, position those notes as close to the camera as possible, so you'll seem to be looking at/near the camera—even when you're looking at your notes. Rehearse your remarks enough times to have just bullets as notes instead of needing to read from a script.

If you're using slides with notes, it's probably easiest to write your notes into the notes section of the slide program (e.g., PowerPoint, Google Slides, or Keynote) and then use the Presenter View to read your notes. Google Slides makes it easy to move your notes close to the camera, but PowerPoint has them further down the screen by default. You can adjust the sliders on the Presenter View to bring the notes section higher up.

Lighting

When the pandemic pushed us all online in 2020, some professional speakers invested thousands of dollars in setting up home studios with green screens and lights, maybe even including a hair light (that's a real thing). This book was written for presenters who haven't done that in the last three years. Let's review how you can improve your setup without making a considerable investment.

The main thing you need to remember is *Lights! Camera! You!* This means the light source needs to be in front of your camera, not behind you. If you have a window or other light source behind you, you'll be backlit, which could result in a silhouette.

FIGURE 2.4. The light source should always be in front of you to avoid being backlit.

If you have a window on your right side and the sun is streaming in, you'll end up with a shadow across the left side of your face. Blocking your window with shades or curtains is the way to avoid this. Put aluminum foil on the window if you still see the light coming through the shades. Once you've removed the natural light, you can control the lighting using lamps.

If you have a darker skin tone, you'll need a bit more light in front of you. Be cautious about being washed out by too much light if you have a lighter skin tone.

Facing a window is generally a good idea, except when the sun moves during your meeting. Suddenly, you have vertical lines from the blinds across your face. If you're facing a window, use sheer or other soft light window treatments instead of shades.

Never rely on natural light as your only light source. You may need to present on an overcast day or at night. Speaking of light sources, here are some ways to set up your lighting:

- Two lamps on either side of your monitor angled toward you. This will cast an even glow on both sides of your face and minimize glare if you wear glasses.
- A small ring light about six inches above your camera makes it easier to look directly at the camera without staring at a light.[3]

If you're using a ring light of any size, make sure there's nothing reflective behind you (such as framed art with a glass cover), or your audience will see the ring lights in the reflection.

Video Framing

Imagine for a moment that you were invited to do a virtual interview on MSNBC or CNN. Would you change anything about the way you're currently presenting on Zoom?

Let's treat every opportunity to present virtually as a big media moment. For starters, no more staring down at your laptop camera at an awkward angle so we can see your ceiling. No one looks great from that angle. We can all do better.

One of my biggest pet peeves is something I call "shrimping." Speakers who sit so low on their screen that their Zoom name runs across their chin when they share their screen. Above them is empty air for half the screen. They look like Wilson, the sweet and mostly unseen neighbor on *Home Improvement*![4]

FIGURE 2.5. and FIGURE 2.6. If you sit too low and share your screen, your name will cross your chin.

Body position can affect how people feel and how they're perceived. You've heard the phrase "walk tall" or that the "Superman pose" fuels confidence.[5] Well, I'm here to tell you that's just as important when you're presenting (or even participating) on a Zoom call.

Here's how to properly frame your video:

1. Sit up nice and tall in the middle of your screen.

2. The camera should be at eye level.

   - Are you using a laptop? Put your laptop on a few books or a box to raise your camera to eye level.

   - Are you using a desktop? You may need to sit on a cushion if you need to look up at an angle to look at your camera.

3. Move the screen, so it's about an arm's length away from you.

4. If using a laptop: Tilt your laptop cover toward you to remove the large gap above your head (we should not see your ceiling!).

5. Leave two fingers of space above your head.

FIGURE 2.7. An example of how to properly frame your video.

That's it. Doing these five steps will put you heads and shoulders above most people presenting on Zoom (pun intended). If more than one person is presenting, try to position each speaker similarly so their shoulder height and the amount of space above their head match. Think about how a panel looks on CNN or MSNBC. No matter how tall each panelist is in real life, every panelist is positioned the same on the screen, so they line up when multiple panelists are visible.

Virtual Backgrounds Dos & Don'ts

Not all virtual backgrounds are created equal. When done poorly, they can distract from your message and make you look like an amateur. Whenever possible, I recommend using a physical background, meaning a wall with a bookshelf or a wall with a piece of art. I understand that's not always possible, so let's look at your options and how to select a virtual background.

Unfortunately, the virtual background images you'll find on websites that curate images have many options that aren't right for a professional presentation.[6] It's understandable that Zoom users are confused about what constitutes a quality virtual background for a professional purpose, since the first three images that Zoom gave us were the Golden Gate bridge, a field of grass up close, and a view from space.

Keep this in mind as you select a virtual background:

- Using a green screen and proper lighting will reduce the fuzzy outlines around your hands and hair.

- Darker backgrounds work better than lighter ones without a green screen.

- Text/logo should be in the top right or left corner of your Zoom video, not behind your head.

- If the text looks backward, it's because you're mirroring YOUR view, but participants will see it correctly. Do *not* flip the image before uploading.

- If you have curly hair, you're bald/balding, or you have gray or white hair, virtual backgrounds may not work well without a green screen.

- Your device must meet minimum requirements to display a virtual background image or video.[7]

- A blurred background is a good option if you can't find a suitable image and want to obscure your physical background.[8]

A beautiful photo isn't necessarily a good option for a virtual background while you're presenting. For starters, if the goal is *not* to draw attention to your virtual background, choose an image that could be your home or office. That means an interior image, not nature, travel, or art.

Here are other considerations to keep in mind when selecting a virtual background image:

FIGURE 2.8. No images with people in them.

FIGURE 2.9. No images with a visible bed. Use a virtual background to hide your bed!

FIGURE 2.10. No images with a laptop or computer (why would you sit with your back to a computer?).

FIGURE 2.11. Avoid clutter or lots of furniture, art, or books.

FIGURE 2.12. AND 2.13. Avoid images with an odd perspective.

FIGURES 2.14. AND 2.15. No images with something poking out from behind your head.

FIGURE 2.16. Notice anything wrong with this virtual background? I didn't catch it at first.

FIGURE 2.17. It's surprisingly difficult to find a decent image on sites that promote themselves as a virtual background image resource. Here's an example that meets the criteria I listed above.

Another option is to create your own virtual background. This would allow you to add your own branding. Stick with darker colors (e.g., blue instead of white), and make sure your logo is in a top corner, not across the entire screen.

Logos as Virtual Backgrounds
Upload your logo so it fills the screen rather than being only in one corner. When you select this image as your virtual background and cover your camera, the result will be a full screen image displayed rather than the smaller one showing when you turn off your camera. This is an excellent option if you want to spotlight someone while a video is playing, but you don't want to have everyone watch that speaker watch the video. Instead, switch your virtual background to the full-screen logo, cover your camera, and spotlight yourself.

Camera

Are you using a laptop when presenting? If your laptop is more than a couple of years old, you probably don't have the best camera. Suppose I had access to only my 2018 MacBook Air in March 2020. In that case, I don't think I could have built a successful business as a virtual event design consultant and executive Zoom producer because the video is dark and grainy, no matter how much light I have on in the room.

If you're being paid to speak virtually, you may want to invest in a desktop computer with a higher-quality camera or purchase an external camera.

A desktop computer would commit you to using the same setup every time you present, which is one way to improve your A/V setup. If you know you'll be speaking from a specific room in your home every time, you can work on creating a better physical background. For instance, I purchased reclaimed wood wall panels to improve my background and added a ladder shelf and a snake plant.[9]

FIGURE 2.18. I made several office upgrades once I had a permanent location for my presentations.

When it comes to external cameras, Logitech cameras stand out among professional speakers—especially the Brio 4K ($129), Brio 501 ($129), and C920x ($59).[10] One of the questions is whether you need 4K video or will 720p suffice. If you're creating professional videos from your virtual presentations (e.g., a speaker reel), 4K may be better, but it will also require more bandwidth, and the recordings will be larger files. New camera models are always coming out, so comparison shop before committing to a model.

If you're using an external camera, check out PlexiCam.[11] This ingenious device allows you to place the external camera anywhere on your screen to make "eye contact" with your audience more easily. The device is transparent, so you can still read your notes or see your slides, but the size of your external camera will impact what parts of your screen are not visible.

There is also an option to use your mobile phone camera via Camo by Reincubate.[12] I used this with a small phone stand while traveling with my laptop.[13] I placed the camera (i.e., my mobile phone) just above my laptop at the perfect eye level without putting my laptop on any books or a box. This setup would also work well with PlexiCam, as they have a model that holds mobile phones.

Audio

As important as the other five topics are, nothing will make participants leave your Zoom meeting faster than poor-quality audio. Our brains can fill in video glitches without too much difficulty, but when audio is choppy, fuzzy, or hard to hear, our brains want to quit.[14] If participants do stick around, research shows that your message will become less credible, and you'll be perceived as less intelligent and less likable. Ouch.[15]

Several microphones on the market come highly recommended by professional speakers and podcasters, including what I use: Heil PR40 (microphone $350, complete set up ~$700)[16] and these microphones: Shure SM7B ($399),[17] Shure MV7 ($249),[18] Blue Yeti ($99).[19] That's quite a price range, so you'll need to research what would meet your needs.

If you're concerned about background noise (kids, pets, neighbors, ambulances, etc.), try Krisp.ai.[20] If the problem continues, you may want to invest in the Heil PR40. I purchased this microphone in 2015 when I started recording podcast interviews. I was living in the staff apartment of a college dorm building, and across the busy street was a hospital. It was always noisy when I was recording, but the Heil PR40 blocked all that out. I now have a home office with many hard surfaces, plus loud kids, and I never have to worry about background noise.

Other simple ways to improve your video and audio:

- Lock your office door, so you're not interrupted.

  Little kids can't read signs, so make sure they know you can't be disturbed. With that said, your participants will hopefully understand if you're the only adult at home and you're interrupted by little ones.

- Remove pets from your office.

  I had someone record a podcast interview with two large dogs in the room wearing loud chains. Not a good plan.

- Use an Ethernet cord rather than wifi.

  If you must use wifi, sit as close to the router as possible (within ten feet), with no walls in between. To increase your bandwidth, ask everyone else in your home to refrain from using the internet. This is one of the reasons we still have a DVD player!

TETHER PHONE AUDIO WITH VIDEO

If you're presenting and your computer audio isn't working correctly, you can switch to using your phone audio without logging into Zoom a second time.

To start, find the mute button on the bottom left of your Zoom window and click on the ^ next to it. Then select **Switch to Phone Audio**, dial one of the numbers, and carefully follow the prompts. You will be asked to enter the **Meeting ID**, your **Participant ID**, and the meeting **Passcode**. All this information is visible on the pop-up window after selecting **Switch to Phone Audio**.

Following these steps also means your video and audio will be linked when you're sent to a Breakout Room, so your audio isn't sent to Room 3 and your video to Room 7.

SETTING UP YOUR DESKTOP

Have you ever rented a car? When you first get into the driver's seat, you need to make adjustments so the car feels right. You might adjust the mirrors, the seat, and even the steering wheel's angle. The same happens when you switch from working on your computer to using that computer to present on Zoom.

POP OUT CHAT

By default, Zoom merges the **Chat** and the **Participant** list to the right side of the Zoom window, with **Participants** on top and **Chat** on the bottom.

Prefer to have these windows floating instead of attached to the Zoom window? You can. Click on the down arrow on the top left of either window and select Pop Out.

To reattach these windows, click on **Merge to Meeting Window** (for Chat, click the **three dots (. . .)** at the bottom of the window to find this option).

Using a mouse with your laptop may make it easier to navigate quickly from one window to another on your desktop.

Here's a checklist that will help you get your computer ready for a presentation:

The Day Before

- Check for updates to your Zoom desktop client (a.k.a. the Zoom computer app). Need some help? Watch a video at www.robbiesamuels.com/updateZoom.

- Restart your computer. If you wait to do this right before joining Zoom, you might have several computer updates that delay joining your meeting.

That Day

- Close browser tabs that you don't need.
  (TIP: Use www.one-tab.com to close Chrome tabs quickly.)

- Join the Zoom meeting.

  1. If you're not the **Host**, ask to be a **Co-Host**.

  2. Exit full screen Zoom (if applicable).

  3. Open the **Participant** list and pop it out. I recommend moving it to the top right of your screen.

  4. Open the **Chat** window and pop it out. I recommend moving it to the bottom right of your screen.

  5. Reduce the width of the Zoom window and place it just below the camera.

  6. Are you referring to notes? Move them as close to the camera as possible.

  7. Are you referring to an agenda or other material? I recommend placing this on the left side of your Zoom window.

  8. Enable **Captions** (you can then hide captions if they distract you.)

I'm right-handed, so my placement recommendations relate to the Chat and the Participant windows being close to the mouse I'm using. You do you. Decide what feels best and create a routine, so you always set up your desktop the same way before each presentation or event you host.

WHY OPEN THE PARTICIPANT WINDOW?

Why open the participant list? With the **Participant** window open, you can easily let participants in from the waiting room, call on participants in the order that they raised their hand, see results of nonverbal feedback (green check mark/red x), clear feedback, call on participants in alpha order, and mute individual or all participants.

Stop Going Full Screen

I mentioned this when reviewing the *Zoom Desktop Client Settings* in Chapter 9, but it's important enough that I want to call further attention to this. When you're presenting and Zoom is full screen, you can't easily access the other applications on your computer.

Zoom can't be full screen if you have only one monitor and you want to have your agenda, run of show, notes, or other programs side-by-side with the Zoom window.

You can always hit the escape key to exit full-screen mode, but it's easier to change the settings so Zoom stops going full screen every time you join a meeting or someone else shares their screen.

To start, look on the bottom left of your Zoom window and click the ^ next to **Mute**, then select **Audio Settings**.

Click on General on the top left. On the right side of the next screen:

- Uncheck Enter **full screen when starting or joining a meeting**.

Click on Share Screen on the left menu. On the right side of the next screen:

- Window size when screen sharing: Maintain current size.

Use the Task Switcher

If you use a program like PowerPoint that goes full screen and you need to easily access Zoom again, use **Alt + Tab** on a PC or **Command + Tab** on a Mac. That will bring up a menu of all the open programs on your computer. You can tab from left to right until you reach the program you need.

Now that you're set up for success, it's time to get to the fun stuff *Online Facilitation*, *Session Formats*, *Engagement Tools*, and *Breakout Rooms*.

CHAPTER THREE

Online Facilitation

Online facilitation is a critical element of a quality virtual event experience. Several factors will improve your online facilitation skills: knowing how to hold space, being able to guide participants through an experience, and understanding the Zoom platform.

HOLDING SPACE

For some of the events I produce, there's a need for a facilitator. This person may or may not have expertise on the topic. Often, these are conversation guides assigned to a breakout room, not to share their opinion, but to ensure each participant is invited into the conversation. They may have thoughts to share or a story to tell to ignite conversation, but their primary responsibilities are to ask probing questions, track time, and monitor participation.

> *I believe that facilitation is a function of equitable access. Knowing when and how to participate helps all participants join in the conversation. This is especially true when the topic is an uncomfortable one. Facilitators create and hold a supportive space for understanding and growth. This may not feel like a "safe space," since participants may be outside their comfort zones, but with support, this is where participants will experience personal and professional growth.*

If participants are gathering for a 60 to 90-minute conference session, not as an ongoing class or team, I don't recommend spending time on lengthy participant introductions. This doesn't mean skipping out on an icebreaker entirely. You can kick off the conversation by asking participants to respond to a question in chat or to answer a poll—something that helps them realize they're not the only one in the room a bit outside their comfort zone will help.

Especially in small breakout rooms, it's obvious when participants have their cameras off and stay on mute the entire time. I had to learn that participation is different for everyone, and some people will not be comfortable speaking up in groups—even in a group of 10 people. Invite someone to chime in once or twice, but don't spend a lot of time wrangling people who don't want to be on camera or unmuted. It's possible that some participants were "voluntold" to attend (meaning it was not their choice). Some may be distracted because they're juggling childcare or parent care during the session. Focus your energy on engaged participants while creating opportunities for everyone to respond to prompts in chat.

If there are fewer than 10 participants in the main room or a breakout room, you can invite all participants to unmute unless they have background noise. This will allow the conversation to be more free-flowing with you as the facilitator available to keep the group on topic, and to make sure no one dominates the conversation. Take notice of cues indicating a participant wants to speak. This includes facial expressions (such as a questioning look), unmuting, or a raised pen. Create space for them to join the conversation.

Sometimes, you'll have the opposite problem. A participant will enthusiastically share stories, advice, or give a lengthy background story before asking a question. Later in this chapter, I'll share how to interrupt online if a participant is not monitoring their participation and going on too long.

If it's a larger group, perhaps the main room instead of a breakout room, then everyone unmuted would be chaotic. In that case, it's important to decide on the structure for the conversation (ask participants to queue up using the **Raise Hand** button or to write their questions into chat).

ON DECK METHOD

If you were facilitating group introductions at an in-person event, the order of introductions would be self-evident. If they were sitting in rows, you'd select someone at the end of a row to introduce themselves, and they would pass to the person next to them. Everyone would know when it was about to be their turn. If the chairs are in a circle, to avoid confusion, you'd need to clarify whether the second person to speak will be to the left or right of the first. Occasionally, people sit just outside the circle, which means you need to figure out when to invite them to introduce themselves. But, generally, facilitating the order of group introductions in person is easy.

Unfortunately, we can't apply that same format to a virtual meeting. The order you see on your Zoom gallery view is not the same order participants see on theirs, so participants don't know they're about to be called upon next. Also, the order of videos will shift when participants turn their cameras on and off, raise their hands, or leave and rejoin the meeting. This makes it hard for you to track who has already gone and who's next.

Save Gallery View order

You can rearrange participant videos in Gallery View and save the order. Click and drag any participant video to the location on the screen you want. New participants are added to the bottom right or the next page if there are multiple pages. You can share this new arrangement with participants, so they will see what you see in Gallery View.[1]

When the facilitator's Gallery View order is not visible to participants, this leads to much confusion and delays, because participants are not prepared to unmute and share when you call on them. I've seen participants caught like a deer in the headlights when they're put into the spotlight without any warning and told it was their turn to speak.

Simply put, they're caught off guard, and it's not a good feeling. It's possible they were multitasking or daydreaming, but it's just as likely that on their screen, they're up on the top row next to you. They have no idea that on your gallery view, they're right next to the last person who spoke.

> *If you want participants to be prepared to speak and unmute when it's their turn, you'll need to give them a heads-up.*

For example:

> *"In a moment, you'll each have the opportunity to briefly introduce yourself. We'll start with Amber and continue in alphabetical order. I'd like you to share your name and pronouns (if you'd like) and describe your role at the company. Please limit your introduction to 30 seconds. After Amber, it will be Brian's turn. Please be ready to unmute yourself when it's your turn. Amber, the floor is yours."*

> Amber shares her introduction.

> *"Thanks, Amber. Next is Brian, and then Charlotte."*

Let's break down all the online facilitation techniques used in this example:

- Everyone knows the order will be alphabetical by first name. *This gives participants some sense of whether they'll be going closer to first or last.*

- Amber is told she will be first *before* the instructions are shared. *This allows Amber to pay closer attention to the instructions, something she may have missed if she had only heard her name when it was about to be her turn.*

- It's clear what each person should say and that they should say it in 30 seconds.

  Saying "introduce yourself" without clear prompts and a time limit may not yield the answers you'd like and could lead to three-minute introductions when you only have time for 30-second introductions.

- At the end of these instructions, Brian realizes he's going to go after Amber.

  Even if Brian had been distracted during the instructions, he will listen to what Amber says, so he knows what's expected of him, and he'll be ready to unmute when she's done speaking.

- After Amber speaks, Charlotte is told she's after Brian.

  This means she'll be ready to unmute and introduce herself.

Some prompts would benefit from an example. In that case, demonstrate how to answer the prompts in 30 seconds by answering them yourself before turning it over to Amber.

ASK TO UNMUTE BUTTON

If you don't want to verbally announce who's on deck, you can tell everyone to stay muted until a **Request to unmute** button pops up on their screen. That's their cue to get ready to unmute when the person before them is done speaking, and you tell them it's their turn.

There are two ways to send this button to a participant:

- Hover over their name in the **Participant** list, click on the **More** button, and select **Ask to Unmute**.

- Hover your cursor over their video and select the **Ask to Unmute** button.

Alpha order

Open the **Participant** list and click on the **Mute All** button.
Everyone is now listed in alphabetical order by first name. As
participants unmute, their name rises to the top of the list, under
the host and co-host names. If multiple participants unmute,
that section of the participant list will list unmuted participants
in alpha order by first name.

HOW TO INTERRUPT ONLINE

If you decide to queue up participants to ask questions via the Raise
Hand feature or ask each participant to introduce themselves, you'll
want to know how to politely interrupt if someone speaks a bit too
long, so you can keep the program on time and on track.

Before I share how to interrupt, let's discuss how to minimize the need
for this to happen by giving clear instructions for when to unmute and
for how long—and how to enforce those instructions.

If you have 12 participants, you might invite everyone to give a 30-sec-
ond introduction before jumping into the content. If you're not careful, that six to eight-minute segment could easily take 15 minutes or
longer, impacting the timing for the rest of your program. To lower
the risk of that happening, use the "on deck" method I describe and be
very specific in your instructions.

For example, "We'll begin with 30-second introductions starting with
Amy. Please say your first and last name so we know the correct pro-
nunciation, share your location, and tell us what you're hoping to learn
today. After Amy, it will be Brian's turn. Remember, just 30 seconds
per person, so we leave enough time for what I've prepared for you."

Amy and Brian follow your instructions perfectly, but Charlie takes
more than a minute—closer to 90 seconds. Dawn will take her cue

from Charlie, so she takes about 75 seconds. Then when Ed starts to go past 30 seconds, you decide to take action and cut him off. Yes, that's interrupting, but it's doing so in a way that causes harm. Ed was following what he saw the previous two people do, so he will feel chastised and personally attacked if he's called out when Charlie and Dawn were not. All participants will be concerned that you'll embarrass them, and this may lead to less engagement during your program for fear that you'll cut someone off unexpectedly.

Let's rewind and try this again.

After Charlie takes too long, take a second to restate the instructions with an emphasis on 30 seconds and the reason you'd like to keep introductions short. Dawn will then keep her introduction to 30 seconds, and Ed will follow suit.

Let's say that you know that Charlie tends to talk a lot. How do you manage his time without embarrassing him? This is where it's helpful to understand how to interrupt politely.

This technique is simple: *Thank You. Thank You. Thank You. Next.*

For example, Charlie shares his name and location, then launches into a story about what he wants to learn, not following the example set by the previous two participants who shared a single sentence to answer the last part of the prompt. As he's speaking, you say phrases like, *"Thank you," "That's great," "I appreciate you sharing that," "Good to know,"* and other positive phrases that acknowledge what Charlie is saying without letting him speak uninterrupted for too long. After using three of these phrases, you interject to say, *"Awesome, thanks. We'll now pass the mic to Dawn."*

These positive interjections allowed Charlie to wind down his remarks rather than ramp up his story. He's unlikely to feel personally attacked because you acknowledged what he was saying before shifting to another participant. Participants witnessing this interaction won't fear you'll embarrass or cut them off, so their willingness to participate won't be diminished.

The sooner you get participants back on track, the easier it is to reset without hurting anyone's feelings or damaging your relationship with participants. Letting participants go on and on hurts your reputation as a facilitator, leading to poorly managed sessions, which waste participants' time and reduce the amount of time available for content and questions.

PARTICIPANT ORIENTATION

Have you ever roamed through a mall, looking for a particular store? That's when it's helpful to locate one of those big maps on a kiosk that shows you where all the stores, food court, and parking are located. Those maps (these days, they're often apps) help you find your way quickly and know exactly where to go. That's called wayfinding, and it's also what your participants need while in your Zoom room.

It is up to you to give them the map they need to find their way around your meeting or presentation–when and how to ask questions, when to expect breaks, and how to interact with you and each other.

Start by including this information at the beginning of your program in a Participant Orientation. Here's an example of what you could cover:

ZOOM ORIENTATION & HOUSEKEEPING

"Before we get started, I'm going to give you a quick overview of how we'll use Zoom and a few other housekeeping notes so you can have a great experience."

- Open the **Chat** window. The **Chat** button is at the bottom middle of the Zoom window.

- When writing a question in chat, please start by writing the word **QUESTION** in all caps, so it's easier for us to spot it.

- If you haven't yet, please update your name to include your pronouns (if you'd like) and your location.

- Hover your cursor over your video and then click on the **three dots (. . .)** on the top right. On the menu that appears, select **Rename**. If you're on a mobile phone or iPad app, click on **Participants**, then your name to rename. I'll paste these instructions into chat for easy reference.

- Click on the **Reactions** button on the bottom right of the Zoom window. This is where you'll find emojis, the yes/no non-verbal feedback options, and the **Raise Hand** button. If you're on a mobile app, this may be under the **More** button.

- In addition to using emojis, we encourage each other by using American Sign Language "applause." [Demonstrate with "jazz hands."]

- We encourage you to have your cameras on, if at all possible. We know our speakers will be more engaging if they have an engaged audience.

- If you're calling in with a phone with no video option, use *6 to mute and unmute; this is especially important when you're in a breakout room. Remember *6. To raise your hand while on a phone, use *9. This also lowers your hand.

> - We will have a 15-minute break at 2 pm and 3:30 pm ET. You'll hear music playing when two minutes are remaining in the break. Please be in your seat when the break ends.
>
> - Lastly, if it's a mealtime in your time zone, follow first-date rules (nothing too messy), and you'll be fine to leave on your camera."

I recommend creating a "You are here" slide that tells participants where you're on the agenda and what's coming up next. My simple design for this slide is a list of topics with a large plus sign next to each one. All of the plus signs are greyed out, except for the topic we're about to begin, which is bright orange. I share an updated version of this slide at least every couple of topics to help reorient participants who got side-tracked or distracted. Neurodiverse participants have told me they appreciate this slide, which helps them re-engage after losing the conversation thread.

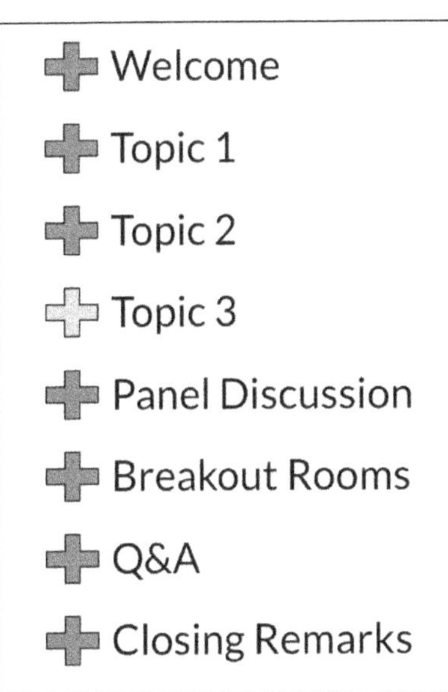

FIGURE 3.1. Example of a "You are here" slide.

A variation of this slide could have the agenda with the time marked, noting when breaks will be. Make sure you keep to those break times, as participants may have planned to be away from their desks. Especially if your participants are working from home, they may have demands on their time that need to be factored into a full-day virtual conference. Knowing, in advance, when the breaks will happen helps them manage their time and be present during the program.

Another consideration is time zones and mealtimes. If you're planning a full-day or half-day event, what mealtimes need to be factored in based on the time zones of your participants? Ideally, provide an extra-long break (45 minutes to an hour) during the time most participants will prepare and eat a meal.

MANAGING Q&A

One of the best ways to demonstrate expertise as a speaker is to decrease the amount of pre-planned content and increase the amount of time allotted to Q&A. Participants perceive speakers as being much more knowledgeable when they answer questions off-the-cuff rather than reading pre-scripted remarks.

I've coached presenters to use a frequently asked question to kick off Q&A or to save a point that would have been shared during the presentation and instead pose it as a question. Doing either helps transition to the Q&A format and gives participants time to share their questions in chat if they haven't been collected throughout the program.

I often include "pause" slides in my presentation to give participants time to jot down their takeaways in their own notes and write their questions into chat. Doing so means I can jump right into Q&A when it's time.

FIGURE 3.2. Example of a "pause" slide.

While Q&A can be a lively and engaging part of a program, too often, it's not. This can be true for in-person and virtual events, but a virtual platform has a distinct advantage—you can screen questions via chat. This means you can avoid the typical first question at an event, which is usually not actually a question, but a comment instead. I'm sure you've experienced this at an in-person event.

The speaker announces it's time for Q&A and invites participants to line up at a microphone to ask their questions. The first person in line is Bob, who doesn't have a question per se, but he does have a story to tell. Politely, the speaker tries to ask Bob if he has a question, but he's too busy putting on a show and won't easily relinquish the microphone to the next person in line.

This could also happen in Zoom if the speaker takes questions by inviting participants to use the raise hand feature. There's no way to know what each participant will say or whether it will be relevant. For this reason, I am a huge fan of collecting questions via chat and prioritizing which ones to answer. This doesn't mean participants never unmute, but they only do so after their question is selected and only if the speaker feels there's a need for more information before answering the question. Screening questions in this way and limiting microphone access for participants allows more questions to be answered.

When questions are collected through chat, the speaker's attention is divided between their notes, the camera, and reading chat. If you're lucky, the speaker will pause several times during a presentation to answer questions. They'll scroll up and down the chat window looking for a question or two to answer before moving on to the next section. You'll hear them mumbling to themselves as they do this.

Early in the pandemic, I was on a Zoom call where the speaker was scrolling through chat, when quietly—but not quietly enough—she read aloud to herself, "Cats? Why are they talking about cats?" and "Is it Instapot or Instant Pot?" Neither topic was relevant to her talk, so her confusion was understandable, but participants didn't need to watch this unfold in the limited time available for questions.

More likely, all questions will be held until the end of the session. Unfortunately, sometimes a question is asked in chat that should be responded to promptly because there's confusion about the content that would ideally be clarified before the speaker moves on. Since keeping an eye on chat is difficult for most speakers, that question won't be seen at the moment, and, worse, may not be seen at all—even when it's time for questions later on.

Often, there isn't enough time allotted for questions, and what little is planned is shortened when the content portion runs long. The session ends abruptly with "That's all the time we have for questions. Thanks and have a good night."

There's a better way to handle questions and support the speaker—ensure there's always another person signed into the meeting to assist them. Depending on how many participants there are and how complicated the run of show is, this could be as simple as having a chat moderator or may require hiring a trained Zoom producer. Either way, the goal is to allow the speaker to focus on their content without keeping an eye on chat and worrying about all the tech.

At the most basic level, the role of a chat moderator is to watch for questions in chat and to copy them to a separate, ideally shared, document (such as a Google Doc). To make it easier to spot questions, I always ask participants to write **QUESTION** in all caps before their question in chat. That way, those comments stand out.

I train my chat moderators to copy the name of the participant who asked the question, not just the text of the question. This takes a little practice, but it's as simple as highlighting the participant's name and their question in chat, then right-clicking to copy and paste (or using **CTRL + C** or **CMD + C** to copy and then **CTRL + V** or **CMD + V** to paste). Having the name with the question allows the speaker or moderator to say that participant's name before the question is posed or answered.

Here's an example. *"Next, we have a question from Sharon Smithers. She asked . . . "* This will get Sharon's attention, and everyone will realize the questions are being asked and answered live—these are not all pre-written questions. Being able to ask questions makes the "live" component of the program more valuable, so it's good to highlight.

Another benefit of having the name attached to each question is that you can reach out after the session to respond to any questions that weren't answered during the program. Sometimes, you don't have enough time to answer all questions; other times, you may choose not to respond because it's a hyper-specific question.

Copying questions from chat to a separate document makes it easier to prioritize which questions to ask during the limited time for Q&A and also which to answer during the content portion of the program. The chat moderator prioritizes generous questions by bolding them. What is a generous question? The answer to these questions would be appreciated by several participants, not just the one who asked the question. In contrast, hyper-specific questions may cause most participants' eyes to glaze over or lead to them multi-tasking, because the virtual session is not keeping them engaged.

Hyper-specific questions also usually require a lot of background information. In contrast, generous questions don't do that because others in the room were wondering the same thing—even if they may have been too nervous to ask for themselves. In that way, asking a generous question is brave. Answering generous questions will likely cover the most frequently asked questions and help participants understand the content better.

If questions are copied to a shared document, the speaker can glance at the questions document at the end of each segment to see if there are any clarification questions or requests to go back to a previous slide. Alternatively, have the speaker ask the chat moderator if any questions should be addressed before they continue. The chat moderator can decide whether to ask any questions or hold them all to the Q&A portion of the program. If the speaker prefers to hold questions until the end of the program, empower the chat moderator to interject if there's any confusion about the content or requests to go back to an earlier slide.

Then, when it comes time for Q&A, have either the chat moderator or speaker read prioritized questions from the shared document. As questions are asked, the chat moderator should remove the bold formatting. To note that the question was answered live, the chat moderator could then italicize the question. This way, any questions that were not addressed live could be answered in a follow-up message to individual participants after the program ends.

This list of questions could also be used to create new blog posts or articles. If there was confusion about the content, collecting these questions helps the presenter edit their presentation and slides for next time.

ENDING STRONG

Rather than abruptly ending by saying there's no more time for questions, build in two minutes at the end of the program for closing thoughts from the speaker. Tell them in advance to plan for this, then say, *"We have time for one more question, and then we'll give our speaker a chance to share their closing thoughts."*

What might they share? The speaker could restate their thesis, highlight their biggest takeaway, or share a resource to help participants implement the content. Make sure the speaker understands that this is *not* the time to share any new content. They'll need to limit their remarks to two minutes or less, since they're all that stands between participants and the next break.

If one of your session's objectives is to inspire participants to take action, set aside time at the end of a session to focus on calendaring, connecting, and collaborating. This could be preceded by a breakout room that asks participants to share what action they plan to take based on what they've learned. Back in the main room, ask participants to share in chat an action they plan to take in the next two weeks to move forward with their plans.

Waterfall debrief

In the *Breakout Rooms* chapter, I explain how to run this as a "waterfall debrief." This gives participants a moment to draft their message without the distraction of reading everyone else's chat messages.

Calendaring—After everyone has hit enter and the chat has been flooded with messages, take a moment to read a few out loud, then ask participants to take a moment to put their action step on their calendar for some time in the next two weeks.

Connecting—Next, invite participants to scroll through the chat looking for messages that resonate with them and encourage them to send a direct message to any participant with whom they would like to stay in touch to discuss how they could support each other's efforts.

Collaborating—Tell participants that you'll be checking in with them two weeks after the event to see if they've had an opportunity to meet up with each other and to find out what collaborations are underway.

Most in-person or virtual sessions do not provide this level of support to participants in achieving the objective of taking action. At best, participants usually leave with a notebook full of notes and then get immediately drawn into the everyday realities that prevent them from reviewing their notes or scheduling time for the next steps. Just reminding participants to schedule a time to review their notes in the next week would be a step towards making the information shared more actionable.

"GO AHEAD AND UNMUTE"

This phrase is quite common and confusing. You've likely heard this phrase and may have even said it yourself. It's usually uttered right after the speaker finishes their presentation, and the speaker is wondering if anyone has anything to ask, "If anyone has any questions, go ahead and unmute."

There's often a short pause, and then more than one person unmutes and begins speaking. Then there's a back-and-forth while the participants try to determine which of them should go first.

Let's imagine this was an in-person gathering of four or more people. At the end of the presentation, you invite them to ask questions and tell them how to do so:

> "Raise your hand if you have a question."

> "Queue up at the mic if you have a question."

> "Write your question on the index card we provided and pass it to the end of your row."

You would not say, "If anyone has any questions, go ahead and start speaking."

We're not trying to replicate an in-person meeting. Instead, we can reimagine it using digital tools. One of the benefits of a virtual meeting is being able to screen questions via chat, but there are circumstances where you'd prefer to have participants unmute to share their questions. In that case, Zoom has a feature to make this process seamless:

> *"If you have any questions, please use the **Raise Hand** feature, which you'll find by clicking on the **Reactions** button on the bottom right of your Zoom window."*

Open the **Participants** list to view the order in which participants raised their virtual hands. Then call on participants in the order they raised their hands.

Combine this with my "on deck" method, and participants will be ready to unmute when it's their turn.

MINIMIZING BACKGROUND NOISE

"Um, I'm hearing some background noise? Could you mute yourself?" Then, 30 seconds later, "I'm still hearing some background noise? If that's you, can you go ahead and mute yourself?"

Hearing this repeatedly is annoying and can easily be avoided. I don't recommend that you ignore background noise because that would be even worse. I've experienced virtual events where the speaker didn't take control when there were problems, and no one else did either.

Before I share three ways you can avoid this distraction, when you're presenting, you need to be sure you are always a Host or Co-Host. If you're not, you will not be able to handle this yourself and will be at the mercy of the Host, who may or may not be savvy enough to manage this for you.

Participants will be appreciative when you smoothly remove these distractions, so we no longer have to bear witness to arguments between parent and child, someone answering their phone and getting into a too-personal-for-work conversation, or even just the ambient noise of a coffee shop.

Mute Upon Entry

Background noise is often caused by participants who don't realize they're unmuted as they join the meeting. When this happens, muting individual participants feels like a game of whack-a-mole.

The simplest way to minimize background noise is to have *all* participants muted as they enter the room. Make this the default via the **Zoom.us Settings.**[2] Search for **Mute all participants when they join a meeting** and enable by moving the switch to the right.

When this setting is enabled, all participants will join the meeting muted and will also be muted when they return to the main room from the breakout rooms.

Mute All Button

Sometimes, previous speakers will forget to mute their microphone and accidentally cause background noise. If you're the speaker, you can quickly remedy this by clicking on the **Mute All** button at the bottom of the **Participant** list window.

Unfortunately, if someone other than the person currently speaking clicks on **Mute All,** they will ALSO mute the person speaking (who may not notice right away that they're muted). For that reason, I recommend that only the person currently speaking use this option.

If you're moderating chat or co-hosting, be cautious about when you choose to use the **Mute All** button. Alternatively, you can hover your cursor over any participant's video and click on the **Ask to Unmute** button.

Disable Unmute

Do you want to be 100% certain that participants will not unmute during a presentation? That's possible. You can remove their ability to unmute by clicking on the **Security** badge on the bottom left of the Zoom window and clicking on **Unmute Themselves** to remove the check mark.

If you want participants to be able to unmute during Q&A later in the program, you'll need to remember to click on **Unmute Themselves** a second time to add the checkmark back. Alternatively, you can hover your cursor over any participant's video and click on the **Ask to Unmute** button. That allows that one participant to unmute while keeping everyone else muted.

Minimize Your Background Noise

If you're concerned about what noises participants might hear coming from your microphone, see the section *Your Audio & Video* to learn how to manage this.

SHARING THE SPOTLIGHT

It's important to keep the participants' experience in mind during your virtual program. One of the ways you can improve is to always put the speaker in the spotlight.

If you miss this step, then everyone will see the **Gallery View** (up to 25 or 49 participant videos on their screen, depending on the device they're using).

It's not a great experience to be watching other participants and only seeing the speaker in a small video. Some participants will know that they can switch to **Speaker View** to make the speaker take up their full screen. They do this by clicking on **View** on the top right of their screen. That will partially solve the problem for that individual participant, but create a new one.

If multiple people are speaking—perhaps an interview, panel, or discussion—the camera will dizzyingly swing from one speaker to another speaker. Sometimes this is every few seconds. This isn't a great experience for participants with **Speaker View.** Any time anyone makes a noise, the camera will switch to that person momentarily before switching to the next person who makes a noise.

Ideally, you would control what participants see, and the way to do that is through **Spotlighting**. Before I explain how to use **Spotlighting**, I will share how it's different from **Pin** because these are often confused.

If you **Pin** someone's video, that video will appear large on your screen, but you won't have changed how anyone else is viewing the **Gallery**. Pin only changes what *you* see, not what *all* participants see.

To change what all participants see, use **Spotlight**.

You can **Spotlight** up to nine videos. The option to **Spotlight** is on the menu that appears when you click on the **three dots (...)** on the top right of your or any other video. Other ways to get to this menu:

- On a Mac, click on a video.

- On a PC, right-click on a video.

- Open the **Participant** list window and hover your cursor over a name until the **More** button appears, and then click the **More** button.

Once you've accessed this menu, the next step is to select **Spotlight for Everyone** for the first person you want to put in the spotlight.

Spotlight will not work if the participant's camera is off, although it's possible to turn off a camera after being put into the **Spotlight**. That participant's photo or their name will be visible until they turn their camera back on.

To add another person to the **Spotlight**, choose one of the ways above to access the menu and then select **Add Spotlight**. Doing this will put two people or more (up to nine) on the screen. Participants will only see the people in the **Spotlight** unless they choose to switch to **Gallery View,** which will only change what is on their own screen.

Spotlight switches to Gallery View

If you remove everyone from the **Spotlight**, Zoom will switch back to the **Gallery View**. This is a change as the default used to be Zoom would continue to show everyone **Speaker View**!

To avoid this, remove all but one person from the **Spotlight** by accessing the same menu on each person's video and selecting **Remove Spotlight**. Then, instead of removing the last person, click on the menu for the next person who should be spotlit and select **Replace Spotlight**. If you follow this process, participants will not see the **Gallery View** in between speakers.

THE FUTURE IS LEFT — MIRRORING ONLINE

One of the reasons participants experience Zoom fatigue is confusing instructions and poor facilitation. That could include saying things like, "Go ahead and raise your hand in chat" when there has never been a Raise Hand option in chat. Another way to cause confusion is by pointing at the wrong part of your screen, saying, "Click on the **three dots (. . .)** at the top right of your screen," while participants see you pointing at the top LEFT of your screen.

You wouldn't purposely point in the wrong direction, so why is this happening?

Within the Zoom desktop client (a.k.a. the Zoom app), a menu includes video settings. To find these settings, click on the ^ to the right of the **Microphone** or **Camera** on the bottom left of the Zoom window and then click **Video Settings**.

The right side of the pop-up window has a live video feed and, below, an option to **Mirror my video**. By default, this is enabled, because we're used to seeing ourselves in the mirror. The live video feed will flip horizontally if you uncheck this option. Check it again, and it will flip horizontally again.

When mirroring is on, any words on the wall behind you will be backward in the video. The same is true if you hold a book up to the camera. When you turn off mirroring, the opposite happens.

*Here's the kicker, **Mirror my view** only changes what YOU see. Participants will ALWAYS see the wording correctly on the wall behind you (or if you hold up a book to the camera).*

Let me say this another way.

You are on a TEDx stage facing your audience. If you move to your right the audience will see you moving to their left.

You are a yoga instructor facing your students. Your students will naturally mirror your movements, so you need to raise your left hand while saying "right" and then raise your right hand while saying "left."

In both of these scenarios, the text on the poster behind you will always be correct, never backward.

Again, no setting in Zoom will make it so that your participants view your video feed horizontally flipped. How they see you if they saw you on the street is how they will see you when you show up on Zoom.

That means that when you raise your right hand, they will see that on the left side of their screen. And when you point with your left hand to the top left corner of your screen, they will see you pointing to the top right of their screen.

Got it?

Ok, let's check.

Make an L with your thumb and pointer finger so your audience will see it correctly. Hold it up high…

Did you use your left hand to make the L shape? If so, it will look correct for YOU but not for your audience.

Make the L shape with your right hand; it will look backwards to you and correct for your audience.

FIGURE 3.3. Using my RIGHT hand, I made an L shape with my fingers. It looks backwards to me, but as you'll see in the next image. It will look correct to participants.

FIGURE 3.4. Still using my RIGHT hand, this is the view participants have. They see an L going in the correct direction.

I know this can be a bit of a brain twister, so you can choose not to use your hands when giving instructions and only verbally describe the steps.

But, if you want to be adventurous and keep getting 5% better, here are a few more ways this shows up frequently during Zoom sessions.

As if you're giving instructions to your participants, point to where the **Reactions** button is on the Zoom window.

Did you use your right hand to point down to the right side of your Zoom window (pointing right at the **Reactions** button on your screen)?

What your participants see: you're pointing towards the **Participants** button on the left side of their Zoom window.

Oops.

You can see how this is confusing for participants. You say one thing and point at another. Their brain has to compensate to figure out what you actually meant and if they're not familiar with Zoom they may not find the correct feature, in this case the **Raise Hand** feature under **Reactions.**

Let's try this again.

As if you're giving instructions to your participants, point to where the **Reactions** button is on the Zoom window.

Did you use your left hand to point down to the left side of your Zoom window (pointing towards the **Participant** button on your screen)?

Excellent! You're getting this.

Still confused? Record yourself pointing down as you give instructions and play the video to see whether you're pointing to the correct side of the Zoom window.

Which hand?

For the **Reactions** button, use your left hand to point to the bottom left side of your Zoom window.

For the **Participants** button, use your right hand to point to the bottom right of your Zoom window.

For the **three dots (. . .)** on the top right of Zoom, use your left hand to point to the top left of your Zoom window.

One more important point that will make you a better storyteller on Zoom.

Again, imagine you're standing on a stage in front of an audience, and you're telling a story that has a beginning, middle, and end. To make a stronger impact, you would divide the stage into thirds and stand at one end of the stage when you begin the story, move to the middle, and finally end on the opposite side of the stage.

The question is, what side of the stage should you start on? Stage right—which is YOUR right as you face the audience. Why? Because when you're standing stage right, the audience will see you on the left side of the stage.

From the perspective of our audience, the future is on their right and the past is on their left. Since you're mirroring them, you need to switch that around so the future is stage left (your left) and the past is stage right (your right).

Let's take this back to Zoom.

If you're telling a story that has a beginning, middle, and end or a past, present, and future—where should your hand start?

Hold up your hand to where you would start your story.

Did you raise your right hand? Great! You've got this. Did you hold up your left? Ok, let me share one more example to see if this makes sense.

Your story includes a chart that has started low on the left and gone up, up, up, and to the right. It's a huge success, and you can't wait to tell everyone.

If you didn't get mirroring right as you use your hands to tell this story, it wouldn't make as much sense to your audience. Your inclination is to use your left hand to start low and to the left and then bring it diagonally up and to the right, but participants would see the opposite: you demonstrating a chart that started on the bottom right and backwards up and to the left.

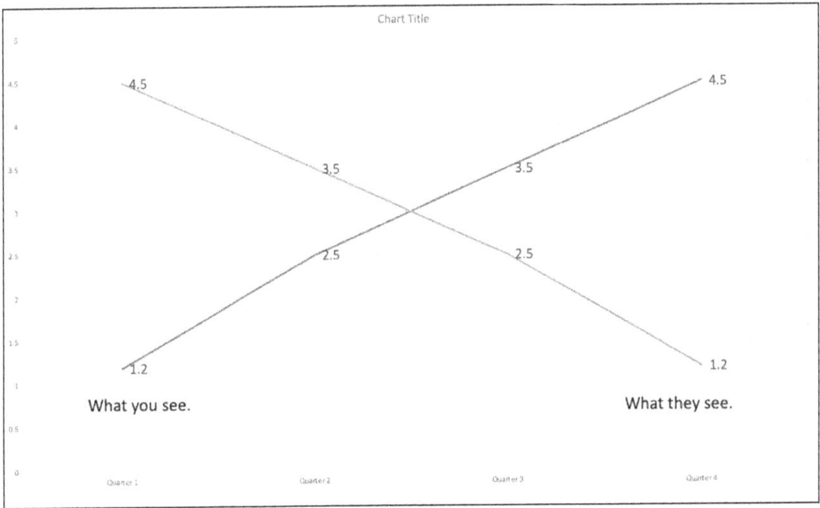

FIGURE 3.5. Demonstrating how hand gestures are mirrored on Zoom, even if you turn off Mirror my image. You want participants to see the chart going up, up, up!

The correct way to demonstrate this chart with hand motions is to start with your right hand low and to the right and then bring it diagonally up and to the left.

If you read through all of this and didn't hold up your hand, I recommend going back and trying all of the exercises.

Put a note on the LEFT SIDE of your keyboard or monitor that says "FUTURE RIGHT" so you remember which hand to use each time and stop confusing your participants.

ZOOM CHAT

Effective use of chat can dramatically change the dynamic of a virtual event. Participants feel heard, and speakers know what content resonated. Unfortunately, this feature's potential is often squandered by poor event design.

Before the pandemic, it was quite common for speakers to open their webinar (and it really was usually a webinar, not a Zoom meeting back then) and ask participants to write their location in chat. This confirmed for the speaker that participants knew where to find chat and since it was a webinar, this was what passed for engagement.

Too often, during these virtual sessions, no one was moderating chat outside of the few moments the speaker asked for these kinds of prompts. That left participants feeling frustrated, especially when they were asking time-sensitive questions or pointing out technical issues. Imagine how it feels to watch a video with no sound, yet no one is paying attention to chat, so attempts to get the event organizer's attention fails.

If the event is being held in a Zoom meeting, I recommend asking participants to update their Zoom name to include their location (and pronouns if they'd like), rather than having them share this information in chat. Why? Information shared via chat flies by so quickly that most participants don't even see it. Discovering something in common is a great way for participants to find a connection. Having this information available on the Zoom display name and chat name makes that easier to do. This is especially true if the Zoom meeting includes break-out rooms. The Zoom display name is like a name tag that will follow the participant into the breakout room. For this reason, you may want participants to put their organization, job title, region, sector, or favorite holiday food after their first and last name. Pick a prompt that connects with your event theme or will help your participants fulfill one of the event goals.

Another common technique is to ask participants to type into chat a letter that corresponds to one of four answers to a question. The chat fills up with A, A, B, C, A, D, C, A, A, B . . . and so on. A better design would be to use a poll to capture this information. For one, using a poll would be a change of pace for participants, and that helps re-engage their attention. Also, answers shared in chat can't be tabulated, so you won't know what percentage of participants answered A or B. That information is easily gathered when using a poll. This does mean planning ahead, so the poll is uploaded and ready to go in the Zoom account.

A yes/no question asked by the speaker is also not a good time to have participants write yes or no in chat for similar reasons as above. There's a non-verbal communication feature built into Zoom that creates a live tally. Click on the **Reactions** button on the bottom of the Zoom window, and you'll see a green check mark and a red x. (Not seeing this? The **Settings** chapter explains how to enable this in the **Zoom.us Settings**.)[3] The green check mark indicates yes and the red x is no. Any host or co-host with the **Participant** window open will see a live tally of these answers, and a checkmark or x icon will appear on each participant's video, depending on how they respond. I share more details about this feature in the **Engagement Tools** chapter, including how to clear participant responses.

I've had prospective clients tell me they want to turn off chat because it's a distraction. When I probe to learn more, it turns out they haven't been doing a good job managing chat and don't see the value of giving participants a way to communicate during the presentation. A speaker told one organization I know he couldn't keep an eye on chat while presenting, so the organization thought the answer was to turn off chat. This is solving the wrong problem. As I mention in the section *Working as a Team* below, assigning someone to moderate chat effectively should be built into the plan from the start. That's the only way to be responsive to participants when a comment or question needs to addressed right away.

How to leverage chat

The chat feature allows extroverts to share their thoughts without interrupting the flow of the meeting by unmuting. It gives introverts a way to jump into the conversation without having to interject to take control of the microphone. It's also a great way for speakers to share additional resources and for participants to stand out by typing into chat their takeaways and links to resources mentioned by the speaker.

I recommend that speakers or the host prep resources that will be shared in chat in the Run of Show or a separate document. This way, you (or your chat moderator or producer) can copy and paste the text with ease at just the right moment instead of worrying about typos while quickly typing a link into chat. Always include **http://** before any link you write or copy into chat, so it becomes a clickable hyperlink rather than plain text. This makes it easier for participants to open the resource in a browser tab during the meeting.

If you have a document you want to send to participants, share it via the **File Transfer** feature in chat. The file can be on your computer, or you can share from several third-party services (such as Dropbox or Google Drive).

Plan to spend a moment guiding participants through how to access the file. They will need to click twice—once to download it to their computer, and a second time to open the file. Don't see the file transfer option on the bottom of your Chat window? The icon is a piece of paper with a corner folded over and it's to the left of the smiley face emoji menu icon. If it's missing, enable this option at **Zoom.us Settings**.[4]

If you've updated your Zoom version to at least 5.13.0, you'll be able to enable the new meeting chat experience at **Zoom.us Settings**. This will allow you to delete chat comments, see the preview of an image in chat, use rich text formatting (bold, italics, bulleted lists) to make your chat comment stand out, share screenshots to clarify your message, quote someone else's comment, reply directly to any message in a thread, and—similar to iPhone text—use an emoji to react to a specific comment in chat. To explore the formatting options, click on the pencil icon on the bottom left of the **Chat** window. To the right of that icon is the screen capture icon. To the right of that is the file transfer icon. The fourth icon is the emoji menu smiley face icon.

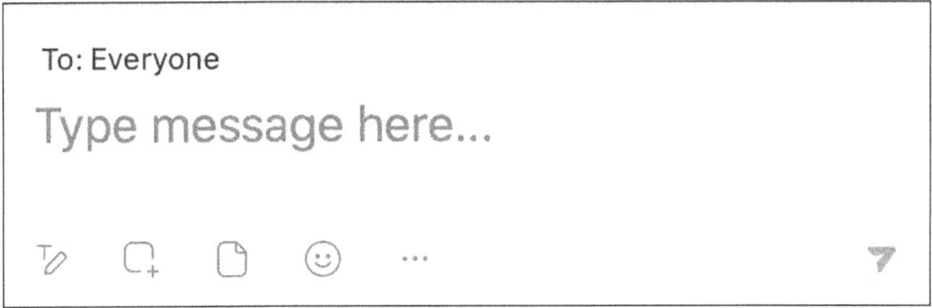

FIGURE 3.6 Chat now has several new features that you access through the icons on the bottom of the Chat window.

While some of these new features are nice to have and can create a more interesting meeting experience for participants, the ability to delete is invaluable. In the *Safety & Security* chapter, I mentioned various ways to lock down your Zoom settings to prevent 'Zoom bombers' from disrupting your meeting. If you don't enable these new chat features, you'll be leaving chat vulnerable. If someone writes an inappropriate comment in chat that's against your community's standards for good conduct, you wouldn't want that message to stay visible in chat after you remove the disruptive participant from the meeting. With these new chat features, you can simply delete the message. It's also handy to be able to delete a message if you have a typo or forgot to put **http://** in front of your link to make it a clickable hyperlink.

Working with youth?

It's possible for one participant to send inappropriate comments to another participant privately, and then delete that chat message so it can't be screenshot and reported. Being able to format text may also cause a distraction. For that reason, it may be best to not enable these new features if this may be a concern for your audience.

In the section on *Managing Q&A* in this chapter, I share how to use chat to screen for the highest priority questions. Highlight both the name of the participant and their message, then use keyboard short-cuts (**CTRL + C** or **CMD + C** to copy and **CTRL + V** or **CMD + V** to paste), or right-click to copy and paste the text into a shared document (such as a Google document).

If you close the chat window while presenting, you'll still see the chat message preview pop up each time someone posts a comment in chat. If you find this distracting, click on the ^ to the right of the **Chat** but-ton on the bottom of the Zoom window and uncheck **Show Chat Pre-views.** If you do, you won't know if there are new messages in chat unless you opened the **Chat** window.

As I mention in the *Setting Up Your Desktop* section of the *Settings* chapter, the **Chat** window doesn't need to stay attached to the right side of your Zoom window. It can be popped out to be moved any-where on your screen. It can also be resized to be wider or taller. Click on the down arrow on the top left of the **Chat** window and select **Pop Out**. To reattach chat, click on the **three dots (. . .)** at the bottom of the **Chat** window and select **Merge to Meeting Window**.

Increase font size in chat
Do you like to glance at chat while presenting? Increasing the font size will make that easier. Click in the **Chat** window as if you were about to type a message. On a PC? Hold down **CTRL** and press the + button to increase the font size (and the - button to decrease it). On a Mac? Hold down **CMD** and press the + or - keys to adjust font size.

Quite often, chat ends up filled with a mix of resources, random asides, and contact information. Saving the chat to review after the event could be useful for you as the speaker and for your participants. To do so, click on the **three dots (. . .)** at the bottom of the **Chat** window and select **Save Chat**. Click **Show in Finder** to open the **Documents** folder with this text file. If you click **Save Chat** again during the same meeting, it will save over this file, so you'll end up with only one complete file, not several partial files.

Some organizations, such as US-based healthcare organizations, don't allow messages in chat to be copied or saved due to HIPAA regulations that protect patient privacy.[5] If you don't have the ability to save chat, that may be why, as it is otherwise enabled by default for all accounts.

In the chapter on *Breakout Rooms*, I share several debrief techniques that leverage chat, including the waterfall debrief, which gives partici-pants a moment to draft their comment in chat before hitting send. It's also helpful to post the prompt or question into chat before sending participants to their Breakout Room. Tell participants to open chat to read the prompt if they have forgotten it.

Chat disappearing

As I was writing this chapter, Zoom was dealing with a bug likely caused by the new chat experience they'd just released. For some Zoom users, messages posted in chat while in the main room were deleted when they went into a breakout room. The good news is that you can Save Chat before entering a breakout room and then Save Chat again later in the meeting—and the file will contain ALL the chat comments, including the ones that are no longer visible in the meeting. You can actually open the chat file in the meeting by clicking Show in Finder after saving chat if you need to find a comment that had been posted before you joined a breakout room.

The host can decide whether participants are able to message all participants, message all participants and each other directly, only contact the host and co-hosts, or not have the ability to comment in chat at all. This can be set by default in **Zoom.us Settings** or adjusted for each meeting by clicking on the **three dots (. . .)** on the bottom of the **Chat** window and changing the selection for Participant Can Chat With.[6]

If community building is one of your event goals, at the end of your event, invite participants to share their contact info (such as a LinkedIn link) into chat and then remind them to save the chat.

IS CHAT PRIVATE?

Zoom used to call messages sent between two participants a "private" message. They switched to calling it a direct message, and that's an important distinction. If a participant sends a direct message to another participant, the host cannot view that message. However, if either participant saves their chat, the direct message will be in the text file. If that direct message is not deleted before sharing this chat file publicly, the message could be viewed by someone else. This is a good reason to follow the advice, "Don't say anything if you have nothing nice to say. And if you do, don't use last names."

Seriously, though, because of the distinct possibility of posting a direct message to everyone instead of one participant (this definitely happens!) and the possibility of a direct message being saved and shared widely—**do not** rely on chat for sensitive messages. If you're the host and intend to share the chat after the event, take a moment to delete any direct messages from the text file first.

Auto-save chat

Have you ever forgotten to save chat? Whether you're the host or a participant, there's a **Zoom.us** setting that enables auto-saving chat. This is particularly helpful if you often remember to save chat in the middle of a meeting, but not at the end, which would mean you'd be missing vital information that was shared in chat during the second half of the meeting.

WHY USE THE WAITING ROOM?

Imagine that you're a teacher, and you're getting ready for class to begin. You'd want your students to wait in the hallway if the door was closed, so you can finish setting up before they enter. Once ready, you'll prop open the door and wave in the students waiting in the hallway. Any students who arrive after the door is propped open will walk right in.

That's why I have the waiting room on by default for all of my meetings. I can always choose to disable the waiting room as soon as I start the Zoom meeting, but if I need a few extra minutes, I'll be able to metaphorically keep the door closed.

I use that time to get settled into Zoom before participants join. If I have speakers, I use this time to review the Green Room Checklist and do a final review of the run of show with them before participants join. (I share this checklist in the *Speaker Checklists* chapter.)

To disable the waiting room, click on the **Security** badge on the bottom left of the Zoom window and click on **Enable Waiting Room** to remove the check mark. Then click on the **Participants** button on the bottom left of the Zoom window and select **Admit All** from the top right of the **Participant** window.

The order of operation here is important. If you **Admit All** from the **Participant** window *before* you've disabled the waiting room, you may inadvertently leave someone stranded in the waiting room because they entered after you clicked **Admit All,** but before you disabled the waiting room. So, first disable the waiting room under the **Security** badge button. Second, click **Admit All** on the **Participant** window.

Can't disable the waiting room?
To close (disable) the waiting room during a call, you need to have a passcode set for that meeting link. This is a step I outlined in the *Scheduling a Zoom Meeting Guide PDF*. To make it easier for your participants, embed the passcode in the link. I explain how to do this in the #NoMoreBadZoom Settings Checklist PDF. Download both of these resources and more at www.robbiesamuels.com/breakout.

Customize the Waiting Room

Being able to customize the waiting room is yet another reason I recommend paying for a Zoom Pro account if you aren't already a user in a Business or Enterprise Zoom account. To get started, go to **Zoom.us Settings**[7] and scroll down a bit as waiting room settings are near the top of the page. Select Customize Waiting Room and you will see the following options:

Change the title message

By default, the waiting room screen displays this text: **Please wait, the meeting host will let you in soon**. You can edit this text (for example, *Welcome! We'll get started in a few minutes.*). The meeting topic (what you named the meeting) will appear if you scheduled a meeting. If this is your Personal Meeting ID (PMI) then it will say **[Your Name]'s Personal Room.**

Add logo and brief message

Another option is to upload a square logo (max 400 px) and write out a description (max 400 characters). This is a branding opportunity. It also allows you to share a brief message with participants while they wait (e.g., *Been in Zoom meetings all day? Take a moment to stretch. Grab a glass of water. Enjoy the silence.*).

Use video

The last customization option for the waiting room is to display the title and upload a video. This is where you can get quite creative. The video can have sound, but it will be muted by default. I add text across my video screen that says, *Help! I'm on mute.* Then I point out where to enable the sound in the bottom right corner of the video. The video will automatically loop. Participants can mute the audio if they don't want to listen to it a second, third, or fourth time while waiting to be let in.

Customization is visible for ALL Zoom meetings
There's no way to customize a waiting room for only one meeting. Put a reminder on your calendar or phone to switch back the waiting room text if you customize it for a very specific meeting.

Participant Order in the Waiting Room

Select the order that participants will appear in the waiting room list. This can either be in the order that they joined or alphabetically. If I want to let a speaker in quickly, I have found that sorting alphabetically makes it easier to notice when a speaker has arrived—especially if they join the waiting room after several participants are already in there.

Renaming in the Waiting Room

You, or a co-host, can rename participants while they're in the waiting room. For example, if you're assigning participants to specific breakout rooms during your program, you may want to put a keyword before their name, so it's easy to identify who will be assigned to each room. If participants are in the waiting room for a few minutes before joining the main room, this might be a good time to rename them.

PROVIDE CLEAR INSTRUCTIONS

As I mentioned, if you're not 100% certain where a feature is on Zoom, write out the instructions in your notes. That will help you avoid saying, "Go ahead and raise your hand in chat," when that feature has never been in chat, and you're confusing your participants. Make your life easier and write out the correct instructions, "To raise your hand, please click on the Reactions button on the bottom right of the Zoom window and then click Raise Hand."

What if you have a participant joining via a mobile app? How do the instructions change? What about participants who join via the web browser instead of an app? The best way to be prepared to guide these participants is to experience this yourself. As a participant, join a meeting from your phone's Zoom app and figure out how to change your name, raise your hand, join a Participants Choose Room breakout room, etc. You'll understand why I suggest that you encourage your participants to always join via a computer—it's a much better interface than the web browser or mobile app.

Tap to join breakout room
If you are setting up a **Let Participants Choose Room** breakout room segment, instruct mobile users to tap their screen to view the **Join Breakout Room** button on the top left of their Zoom app.

FIGURE 3.7. The mobile app no longer has all options hidden under the **More** button. Now there's a toolbar on the bottom that spans two screens. Participants will find **Meeting Settings** and **Background & Effects** under the **More** button. The host will find those, plus **Security**, **Polls/Quizzes**, **Live Stream**, and **Focus Mode**.

Host cannot launch breakout rooms from a mobile device
If you're planning to host a meeting using your mobile phone or iPad, plan to make someone else co-host so they can launch and manage breakout rooms, as there's no **Breakout Rooms** button on the mobile device toolbar.

WORKING AS A TEAM

Whether or not you hire a professional Zoom producer, if you have more than 20 participants, I don't recommend you try to handle everything yourself. If you're the one presenting content, several other roles can (and often should) be filled by someone else.

If you were invited to speak at an in-person event, you wouldn't be in charge of setting up the chairs, ordering catering, managing the A/V setup, promoting ticket sales, or even putting a bottle of water on the lectern before your presentation.

As a virtual speaker, you may have had to play a larger role in the event, including figuring out a professional A/V setup yourself, creating an appropriate virtual stage, teaching others how to load your polls or spotlight you, and, of course, making sure there was something to eat and drink nearby.

If you're hosting a virtual conference or a virtual panel with multiple speakers, there's also the extra effort of making sure these speakers are properly prepped and ready to shine.

Here are the additional roles to be sure to add to your team.

Technical Producer

This is the person who best understands Zoom. They will handle the technical needs of the event, including hosting a speaker prep meeting in advance to be sure speakers have the right setup for their A/V and background, leading speakers through the Green Room Checklist right before the program begins, hitting record, disabling the waiting room, launching polls, spotlighting speakers, sharing slides and videos as needed, and making sure the recordings are sent to whoever is managing the follow-up with participants.

Emcee (or Hand-Off Plan)

How will each speaker know when it's their turn to unmute and speak? While you can write a hand-off sentence into the end of each speaker's remarks (*And next you'll hear from . . .*), an emcee does more than that. They introduce each speaker and at the end of the program, they facilitate Q&A, say thank you to the speaker, and tell participants what's happening next (*Next, we have a 15-minute break. Please stay logged into Zoom and return at 11:15 am ET when we'll hear from our next speaker. . .*).

Introductions

If you choose to create a hand-off plan, you'll still want to have someone assigned to introduce each speaker. This gives the speaker more credibility than if they introduce themselves, and it gives you more control over how much time the speaker spends talking about themselves instead of their content. I share best practices for introductions in the *Content* section of this book.

Q&A Facilitator

If you don't have an emcee role, is there someone else who will feed questions to the speaker? This is especially important for questions that come up during the presentation that should be addressed sooner rather than later. The speaker likely won't be watching the chat closely because they need to be focusing on looking at the camera and glancing at their notes. Some speakers are comfortable selecting what questions to ask at the end of the program if these questions are copied from chat into a separate shared document (such as Google Docs).

Chat Moderator

Speaking of chat, identify which team member will be responsible for keeping an eye on chat, copying questions (and the name of the participant who asked them) into a separate document, and possibly answering simple questions in chat (such as, *what time is the next break?*), and interjecting if a clarification question is asked during the program that needs to be addressed immediately. In the *Online Facilitation* section of this book, I cover best practices for managing Q&A.

Speaker Wrangler

What happens if a speaker is running late or has technical issues joining the call? It's helpful to have someone other than the producer tracking down errant speakers by calling them. (I explain below the need to gather speaker cell numbers ahead of time on the planning document.)

Once all the other speakers are set, the producer can connect with a speaker who is having technical issues joining the meeting, but at least someone else will have found out what the issue was and assured the speaker that this was being addressed. This role should have some basic understanding of what to say if a speaker has no internet or power, so the speaker can start working on Plan B before hearing back from the producer. I cover more about managing this kind of risk in this book's *Safety & Security* section.

Video Editor

Who on your team will make the necessary edits on the video file (editing out the footage before the official Welcome Remarks and removing the empty air during breaks or breakout rooms)? Have you told them what you want to be written on the title slide? Do you want to include graphics on the title slide? What about an end card with contact information for you and your organization?

Social Media and Email Promotion

Who is in charge of thinking about the promotional text and graphics for emails and social media? Will that person also be helping you repurpose the event video for social posts, blog posts, or other resources?

Session Owner

If you have multiple sessions with multiple speakers throughout the day or over several days, assigning one person as the lead for each session is a good idea. Work with them to clarify the purpose of that session and the general flow (such as a 10-minute lecture, 30-minute panel, 20-minute Q&A) before they select speakers for that session.

Virtual Event Design Consultant

This is one of the roles I fill for my clients, helping session owners or individual speakers create a purpose-first design for their sessions. Based on the desired outcomes, I suggest specific content formats and exercises. I also share best practices for opening and closing the session for the greatest impact. Sometimes, this is all I'm asked to do for an event, as the organization has a team to handle the other roles. Other times, I handle this and several additional roles (usually technical producer, emcee, and chat moderator).

> *How are you ensuring all your different team members communicate with each other?*

Run of Show (ROS)

This planning document is the backbone of the event. It's a minute-by-minute accounting of how the event will flow. It includes all the technical cues, introduction text, and speaker cell numbers. This document is where all decisions are committed. No more Post-it® notes with random updates. Mark down all changes on the ROS, so everyone is in the loop.

This means deciding ahead of time how long each segment will be, the order of speakers, and the length of time for each activity. It's not always possible to stick to the ROS perfectly, but creating this structure ahead of time also makes it easier to decide how to adjust the timing if a segment runs over. (Download a sample run of show and other resources at www.robbiesamuels.com/breakout.)

"Just In Case" Text Thread

Send speakers a group text about 30 minutes before the speakers' call time (the time they should be signing in for their pre-event Green Room Checklist). Here's an example:

> *This is Robbie Samuels. I'm producing your Zoom session today. This is a "just in case" text thread. Please reply with your full name. Join us at 11 a.m. ET using the Zoom link in the calendar invite. Thanks!*

Decision-Makers' Text Thread

Separate from the speaker group text thread, set up a communication channel between you and any decision-makers. When I'm the executive Zoom producer, this would mean I set up a text thread with the organization's liaison. It needs to be someone with authority to approve my request to shorten an upcoming breakout room or break to keep the show running on time. Or, if a speaker has severe technical issues, this is who would hear my recommendation for how to proceed and then commit to a plan of action.

While I'm producing the event, I'm doing so on behalf of an organization, so I know I'm not the final arbiter if there are big questions that need answers. I also don't want to have that conversation with all the other speakers in a group text thread. When I'm the presenter, and someone else is producing, I try to set up a direct communication channel with the producer and the client or host.

Recently, this came up when I joined a conference midway through the day, in preparation for presenting the closing keynote. I realized the event was running late. I needed to know how the organization wanted me to handle this. Should I shorten my time to get us back on schedule (the professional option and the one I chose)? Or did they want me to handle this in some other way?

With this team assembled, you will have the support you need to produce an event without stressing about all these responsibilities yourself. If you can think of additional key roles, please share them with me. I'm always looking for ways to improve my clients' experience. Email action@BreakOutofBoredom.com to let me know how this has helped you, and what else you've done to make producing virtual events a joyous rather than stressful experience.

CHAPTER FOUR

Session Formats

While there are several ways we have been connecting and collaborating virtually since 2020, this book is focused on conference sessions. These are usually 60, 75, or 90 minutes and take place as part of a half-day, full-day, or multi-day event or a stand-alone session. This is different from a class or group that is meeting weekly over several months or all year round in an office. It's also different from a virtual happy hour, which has little to no content in the event design. We're focusing here on participants who come together for a one-time experience, where the goal is to create a transformative, engaging, and educational event.

There are three session formats that are the basis of the virtual event designs I create for my clients: Lectures, Fireside Chats, and Panels.

Let's look at each of these.

LECTURE

What do you think when you hear someone is going to give a lecture? My first thought is usually, "Not another death by PowerPoint. Ugh." Sometimes, though, lecture style is the best way to give information to participants. No matter how dry the topic, there are ways to move away from the default of reading slides in a monotone.

Slide Design

For starters, design your slides to have less text and more visuals. Use at least 18-point font. If you can't fit all of your text on one slide using an 18-point font, simplify your message or break it into two screens. You should not expect participants to glean every tidbit of knowledge you provide from your slides. Slides are best when they bring your content to life with images or charts. And . . . slides are not required.

That's right! It would be better, in my opinion, to give an engaging and interactive presentation without slides than to drone on and on reading dense slides. If you're going to use slides and design is not your superpower, it's worth investing in having someone design slides for you. If you'd like to get better at creating slides, try your hand at creating slides using Canva.[1]

Don't Hide Behind Your Slides

If you were presenting in person, the focus would be on you and your slides would be behind you or next to you. When you present on Zoom, you're a tiny box either on the side of the slide or in the top right corner, depending on how your participants have set up their screens. You're definitely not the focus.

Couple this with how few presenters make an effort to look at the camera when they're presenting with slides. Your camera might as well be off for the amount of connection you're having with your audience. I'm not advocating *less* connection. Let's talk about how we can create a *stronger* connection instead.

At the start of your program, address participants by speaking directly to the camera without sharing your slides. This is an often-overlooked opportunity to connect with the audience. Do you really need slides to introduce yourself or tell a story that will captivate their attention?

During the presentation, aside from looking AT the camera as often as possible, another simple solution is to stop sharing your screen now and again, so you're speaking directly to participants full screen. The timing of when to stop sharing your screen to speak to the camera should be planned out as you're designing the session.

If during your rehearsals you find you're spending more than a minute and a half on a slide, you're either reviewing a detailed chart or you're telling a story. If it's the latter, make a mental note to stop sharing the slide after about a minute, so you can finish telling the story straight to the camera.

When it's time to continue to the next slide, simply click on the **Share Screen** button and double-click on your presentation to bring it back up on your screen. With a bit of practice, you may even be able to advance to the next slide before hitting the **Share Screen** button. This would allow you to move on to your next point without having participants re-read the previous slide.

TWO ADDITIONAL WAYS TO NAVIGATE SLIDES

If you realize you're running low on time and need to skip a few slides, don't announce that to your participants, and don't let them see you scroll past slides. Instead, select the **Pause Share** button from the floating toolbar (by default, this is at the top of your screen but can be moved). Pausing freezes the shared screen, so your participants still see the last slide you were showing while you skip a few slides behind the scenes. Select **Resume Share** to show participants the next slide you want them to see.

If you need to switch from PowerPoint to another application (such as a web browser), you don't have to stop sharing your screen. Simply click **New Share** from the floating toolbar and select the window or program you want to share. From the participants' perspective, it will be a seamless transition from PowerPoint to the web browser.

FIGURE 4.1. This floating toolbar gives you access to the Zoom controls while you're sharing your screen.

Avoid these common screen-sharing missteps
When sharing your screen, do not select Desktop. Participants should not be able to watch as you search your computer for a file. Instead, make sure the program or browser window you want to share is already open, and then select that. Click **Share Screen** and look at the options *below* the top row. All of those are individual windows, so when you select one of those, participants won't see anything else on your computer.

Another common mistake is to share **Portion of Screen**. This is a workaround many presenters use, but too often they mistakenly share something they didn't mean to share. I saw a speaker accidentally share a private chat message because the chat window ended up in the portion of the screen that was being shared. Ouch!

PowerPoint Screen Sharing Solution

If you only have one monitor, it can feel impossible to manage slides, notes, chat, and the participant list. It *is* possible, but there's an order of operations to follow as you set it up. The result is that with only one monitor (such as a laptop), you'll share a full screen PowerPoint slide to participants while seeing the PowerPoint Presenter View (with your notes) on your screen. Plus, you can open chat, the participant window, and see five or more participant videos. To make life a little bit easier, have a team member moderate chat.

Here is the order of operations to share PowerPoint

After you join the Zoom call, but before letting participants in from the waiting room:

- In Zoom, click on **Share Screen** and select **PowerPoint** while it's in edit mode.

- At the top of PowerPoint, select **Slide Show,** and on the next menu that appears, select **Presenter View** (this should be the third icon from the left on the second row).

- Stop **Share.**

- Keep PowerPoint open on your computer.

When it's time to present, and you have a *single* monitor:

- Select **Share Screen** and double-click on your slide in presentation mode (not the **Presenter View**). Now participants will see your full-screen slide.

- To see your notes, access the **Presenter View** by clicking on the **three vertical dots** on the bottom left of the slide and selecting **Presenter View.** Now you're seeing your notes, but participants are still seeing your slides.

- (optional) To see **Chat** and **Participant** windows floating on the right side of your screen, open them by selecting the button on the floating Zoom toolbar at the top of your screen.

When it's time to present, and you have *two or more* monitors:

- Select **Share Screen** and then double-click on your slide in presentation mode (not the **Presenter View**). Now participants will see your full-screen slide, and you'll see **Presenter View.**

- (optional) To see **Chat** and **Participant** windows floating on the right side of your screen, open them by selecting the button on the floating Zoom toolbar at the top of your screen.

Download this resource as a PDF and watch the video at www.robbiesamuels.com/breakout.

Zoom window disappeared!
If you click on PowerPoint when NOT sharing your screen, the Zoom window will disappear. To access the Zoom window again, use **CTRL + TAB** (PC) or **CMD + TAB** (Mac) to navigate back to that application. While holding down **CTRL** (or **CMD**), click on the TAB button until you land on your desired application, and then release both keys.

Screen Share and See Gallery View

It's so helpful to see participants react as you present and to tell by their body language whether they're engaged, confused, or tuned out. The default in Zoom is to only show five participant videos whenever you share your screen, although it's possible to display up to 24 participant videos. If you switch to seeing 24 participant videos, it will feel like you're speaking to the gallery view, but for participants, you'll be in the spotlight sharing your slides.

To set this up, at least seven participants need to be in the meeting. Once set up, Zoom will default to this display view every time you share your screen while logged into this particular meeting. You'll need to set this up again if you leave and return.

Here are the steps:

After you share your screen, click on the fourth icon on the top of the vertical strip of videos on the right side of your screen. The icon image is the same as the Gallery View icon—a square made up of nine small squares. Clicking on this icon will change the shape of the six videos from a vertical strip to a 2 x 3 rectangle. Put your cursor on the bottom right corner of this rectangle and while holding down your cursor, pull down and right at an angle. As you do, more videos will become visible. Move this large block of videos anywhere on your screen.

FIGURE 4.2. This fourth icon will be visible at the top of the vertical strip of videos if seven or more participants are in the Zoom meeting when you share your screen.

This is worth repeating from the section about Recording Options & Settings: *If you're BOTH recording to your computer and sharing your screen, the computer recording will show the presenter's video and five other participant videos. To avoid this, record to the cloud with the setting:* **Record active speaker with shared screen**. *Other options are to have someone else record on their computer or have someone else share their screen while you record on your computer.*

SLIDES AS VIRTUAL BACKGROUND

Another way to be a lot more visible when you share your screen is to turn your PowerPoint or Keynote slides into your Zoom background. This allows you to embed your image onto the screen.

Caution: This feature cannot handle any complicated slides, including sound, transitions, or animations—just text and images.

You'll need to redesign your slides to make space for your image. It's easier if you decide you'll always be in the bottom right corner and then design to leave space in that corner.

When you first add a slide deck as your background, it takes a moment to set up (how long depends on the number of slides you're uploading to the background), so best to do this in the green room while participants are in the waiting room.

If you or another participant records this to a computer, the slides will have the speaker video embedded. If you record to the cloud, it will record with the slide next to the speaker video—with the default cloud setting: **Record active speaker with shared screen.**

Pause for Questions and Takeaways

When presenting with slides, it can be difficult to get a sense of how participants are receiving your content. Are they hanging on your every word? Are they still confused by something you said 10 minutes ago?

As you design the flow of your session, consider where you'll pause to invite participants to capture takeaways in their own notes and to write in chat any questions they have. This gives you time to take a breath, drink some water, and glance through what questions have come in so far.

To be certain you have time to present all your modules, you'll likely need to hold most questions until the end of your presentation. If you spot a question that would be helpful to answer right away, do so, as clarifying your point will help all participants stick with you going forward.

To remind yourself to pause, I recommend inserting a pause slide. When that slide is visible, do your best not to speak over it for 30 to 60 seconds. Then address any pressing questions before moving ahead to the next module.

Time for Q&A

A 60-minute session is not 60 minutes of content. At the start of the program, your host organization may use up to five minutes of the allotted time to review the agenda, share a participant orientation, and/or introduce speakers. They may also need a couple of minutes at the end of your time slot to share closing remarks, mention updates, or announce what is happening next on the agenda. In addition, factor in 15 minutes for Q&A that's either all at the end or woven throughout your presentation.

Unfortunately, when time is not managed well, it's Q&A that gets cut. I say, unfortunately, because Q&A is a great opportunity to engage participants. Sharing content without slides is also a great way to demonstrate that you're knowledgeable and not just reading your notes.

If you ask for questions throughout the program, you won't face that awkward moment at the start of Q&A when you're ready to switch gears, but there are no questions in chat. Another way to manage this moment is to eliminate slides for your final two points and instead pose them as questions to kick off Q&A.

For example, *In a moment, it will be time for Q&A, so now would be a good time to write your questions in chat. A couple of questions come up every time I present this material, so I'll kick things off with those since it's likely what many of you are wondering right now.*

If the event at which you're speaking is running late and you're asked to shorten your time, remove one of the modules that isn't critical for the outcome of your session. Do this so you can keep at least 10 minutes for Q&A.

Accessibility and Presentations

Even when you feel you've designed the perfect slide deck, sharing this information with your participants requires a thoughtful presentation. Here are ways to improve your presentation and make it more accessible:

Pause for a moment when you switch to a new slide. This gives participants a moment to absorb what's on the slide before you start speaking. Take a breath, glance at chat, or sip some water—then begin speaking.

Make sure there's contrast between the background color of your slides and the text colors. For example, use a blue background with white paragraph text and yellow titles. Too much contrast (black font on a white background) is hard to read. Check your contrast at https://webaim.org/resources/contrastchecker.

Search for PowerPoint templates with the word "accessible" to find templates tagged as "accessible" by the creator. Additional resources for PowerPoint are available at https://webaim.org/techniques/powerpoint.

The most common form of color blindness is not being able to distinguish between red and green. Avoid using these colors on a chart, because they'll be perceived as shades of brown, which isn't helpful. Add labels to your charts to make the information clearer.

Limit or avoid using animations, GIFs, silent videos, and text swooping in on every slide or as your virtual background. These may trigger migraines, nausea, and dizziness for some participants. Less is more.

Build your slides, so participants don't read ahead and get confused because they're looking at your fourth bullet point while you're still speaking about the second one. Instead of having a slide with five bullet points, start with a slide with just one bullet point. Speak to that point. Then on the next slide (or with a simple transition), add a second bullet. Change the colors of these bullets so the first bullet is now greyed out (or some other low-key color) and the new bullet is yellow (or some other vibrant color). Speak to the second point and then add a third bullet on a new slide (or with a simple transition). Again, grey out the second bullet and make the new bullet vibrant. Follow this pattern as you speak to all five points.

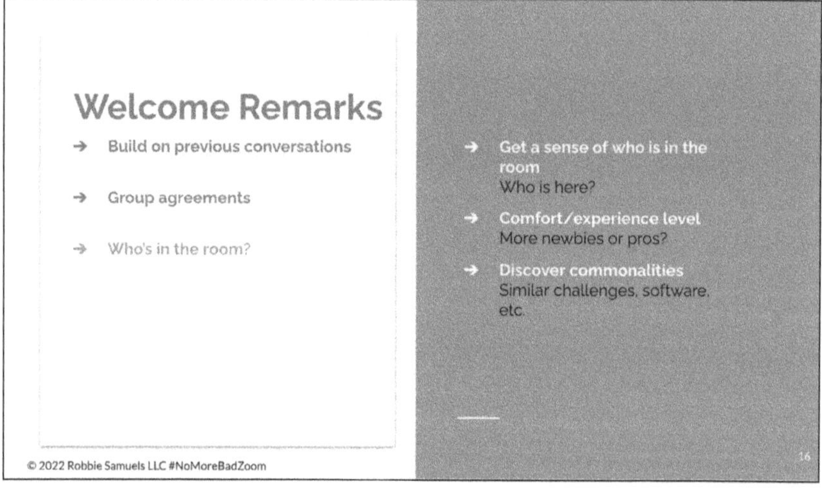

FIGURE 4.3. Example of a slide that builds each bullet. On the left side of the screen, the third bullet is the current point, so it is a brighter color than the previous two bullets. The content on the right side of the screen changes as the slides advance to each bullet.

Don't assume every participant is looking at your slides. A participant may be blind, or they may be multitasking while driving their children to school. Either way, your slides can't speak for themselves. That's your job. Speak to every main point on the slide (which doesn't mean reading the text on the slides, because that will put participants to sleep). Describe any image related to these points. Add the image description to your notes. Rehearse with this in mind.

Ask speakers to take a moment to describe their appearance. Practice doing this yourself: Include information such as gender and/or pronouns (if they're comfortable sharing this), race, and general age (e.g., middle-aged or mid-30s). Race/skin tone is nice to know (e.g., Asian-American, caramel-colored skin, Black). Other details are in the nice-to-know category: glasses, facial hair, shirt color, and any statement accessories (e.g., big earrings, chunky necklaces, unique hairstyles or colors, or funky glasses). If something in your background stands out, that would be nice to know (but only pick one thing to mention). I've been told that if you're sporting purple highlights and a funky statement necklace, you probably don't need to mention anything visible in your background. The goal is to give participants not looking at the screen a sense of who you are and, if possible, a bit of your personality before speaking.

Offer handouts in PDF format and utilize the built-in tool on Adobe Acrobat to make them more accessible to participants who are blind or have low vision.

Include a "pause" slide to give participants an opportunity to catch up with writing their notes or consider if they have questions to type into chat without also having to listen to what you're saying. That requires a level of executive function that can be challenging for neurodiverse participants. As I've mentioned, this could be as simple as a slide with a pause button icon in the middle. Try not to speak for *at least* 30 seconds. Prepare a presentation with less information, so you're not rushing through it and can take a breath, sip some water, and glance at the chat to see if there are any clarification questions to answer before proceeding.

Include a *"You are here"* slide a few times in your slide deck. This helps participants get re-orientated if they got distracted for any reason, including ADHD or other neurodiversity. To create this slide, share your agenda again, clearly marking the upcoming topic. Use a bright color font to highlight the next topic. Mention what's coming up next and, if relevant, when the next break will be.

Enable captions every time. While AI-generated captions are not a replacement for captions typed by a trained professional or a sign language interpreter, there are many reasons a participant would find them helpful besides being Deaf or hearing-impaired. For example, if the meeting is not being held in their native language, if the speaker has an accent that a participant has a hard time understanding, or if reading along helps the participant stay focused.

As I mention in the *Settings* chapter, Zoom has a **Sign Language Interpretation** feature, as well as a **Language Interpretation** feature, that allows live translation into multiple spoken or signed languages. There's also an option to have captions available in more than one language.

Be considerate with your words and avoid ableist terms. For instance, instead of saying "crazy" to indicate something was unexpected or unusual, say "wild." This way, you're not perpetuating mental illness stigma. Another example is saying something is "not cool" instead of "lame." If someone can't walk, they may be lame, but that doesn't mean they're not cool.

Jokes that target differences (e.g., gender, race, body size, disability) could be offensive to your participants and triggering to those with PTSD or with anxiety.

Accept that some participants will have their cameras off. This may be for various reasons, including a neurodivergent participant who finds it easier to stay focused and absorb information without being on camera. This is not a personal slight to you. While I always ask for cameras on, I include a caveat of *"if possible,"* and I don't make it about me if someone chooses to keep their camera off.

Share links in chat at the end. Some participants will get distracted trying to grab links dropped into chat throughout your presentation. They may click on a link and read that resource while you're still speaking. Instead, mention at the beginning of your talk that you'll be sharing links to further resources at the end. I embed a suitcase image onto slides to indicate that I'll share additional resources. I tell participants I've already packed them for you and will give you access at the end of the presentation and in the follow-up email. If you do share links throughout your presentation, tell participants you'll reshare those links in chat at the end of the session or in a follow-up email.

Seek out more information about how to make your presentations more inclusive. My own understanding of this topic is always evolving, thanks to great resources provided by accessibility consultants Donna Mack[2] and Nic Steenhout.[3]

FIRESIDE CHAT

This is an alternative to lectures or panels where you interview one or two panelists. The question to ask yourself is, "Do I need a full panel to help participants think/feel/do something differently?"

This is ideal if you have less time or want to keep participants engaged with different formats. A fireside chat is an interview with one or two people and lasts between 10 and 25 minutes. In contrast, a panel of three people would take at least 30 minutes and often longer.

Here are five reasons to choose this format:

Compare and Contrast

You can facilitate learning around a contentious topic by inviting two panelists to share their views. A guided debate can engage the audience more effectively than stating facts and figures. The stories they share will also be more memorable.

Two Sides to the Story

Invite two people who shared an experience to participate in a fireside chat. Depending on their roles, they may have very different takes on what happened and how it impacted them or their work.

Joint Effort

Invite a representative from two organizations that worked together on a project. Use this as an opportunity to illustrate how their partnership works.

Deeper Dive

Rather than inviting three or more people to share a piece of their story, invite one person who has a great example to share. Use the time to dig deeper into their story and pull out takeaways for participants.

Support a Rookie Speaker

If you'd like to invite someone to speak who doesn't have a lot of experience presenting, this format is a lot easier to prepare for than a 10 to 15-minute talk. Share three questions with them in advance and guide them through a 10 to 15-minute interview.

PANEL

This format is best when participants would benefit from hearing a range of experiences on a topic.

Purpose-First Design

Where would you like each panelist to focus to help participants achieve specific outcomes? For example, if you wanted participants to take a specific action after your session, what's standing in their way? Is it a mindset issue? Do they need help navigating relationships in the office? Are they missing a technical skill?

Ensure that you line up panelists who will speak not just about their amazing achievements but also about how they overcame obstacles. Without that being addressed, participants may see panelists as exceptional and not believe it's possible for themselves or their situation.

How Many are Too Many?

Depending on how long your session is and what you're trying to achieve by hosting a panel, you can expect to have three panelists for a 30-minute module or four for a 40-minute module. What about five? Is five too many? It's not ideal.

Take into consideration how many minutes you'll have available for a panel. If the session is only 60 minutes, then that leaves only 35 minutes for a panel (accounting for a five-minute intro, 15-minute Q&A, and five-minute closing remarks). Is seven minutes per person the best way to have panelists share their experience and move participants to specific outcomes? Probably not.

When there are five or more panelists, it also means that most remain silent most of the time. It's hard to stay vigilant and look like you're paying attention when you realize the moderator is asking each panelist to answer each question for five minutes, and you're six people down the line. I've seen panelists' attention drift off. Some check their phones or seem to be daydreaming. It's not a good look for your participants.

If you have 90 minutes for your session and you need to share a wide variety of perspectives and experiences, consider doing a fireside chat with two panelists for twenty minutes and a panel with three or four panelists for 35 to 45 minutes, instead of six panelists in one 60-minute panel. This fits into 90 minutes, even taking into account the 25 minutes spent on the welcome remarks, Q&A, and closing remarks.

Read on to learn how you can design the panel to be a conversation.

Credibility Introductions

Before we dive into design, let's discuss one of the ways to preserve time for the conversation. Stop handing the microphone to each panelist and asking them to introduce themselves. With even just three panelists, that could take up to ten minutes and it's not the content on which you wanted them to focus.

Instead, have the moderator share a brief introduction for each panelist. That 30 to 60-second introduction should answer two questions that participants are wondering:

"Why should we be listening to this person? And what might we learn?"

That's it. No need to list every book they've ever written or read out all of their degrees. Answer those two questions in the most succinct way possible and design the panel to let panelists shine.

Design for Interaction

Rather than defaulting to every participant answering every question—which can feel tedious even with three or four panelists—prep for a conversation.

As the moderator, meet with panelists ahead of time collectively (if possible) or individually to understand what they can contribute to the conversation and what stories they could share.

With your purpose for this panel top of mind and knowing their answers, determine what questions to ask and who should be the primary and secondary respondents for each question. The primary respondent will have five minutes to share their answer. Then a predetermined secondary respondent will have two minutes to share their additional thoughts—which could be agreements, disagreements, alternatives, etc.

Below, I'll share the prep for three panelists.

- **Question 1**: to panelist A for a five-minute response, and then to panelist B for a two-minute follow-up.

- **Question 2:** to panelist C for a five-minute response, and then to panelist A for a two-minute follow-up.

- **Question 3:** to panelist B for a five-minute response and then panelist C for a two-minute follow-up.

If you do the math, you'll notice that this doesn't add up to 30 minutes, which is the minimum amount of time I said to set aside for three panelists: 60 seconds per panelist for their credibility intros (three minutes), plus seven minutes per question (21 minutes) equals 24 minutes. The additional six minutes are available to you for additional follow-up questions based on what panelists shared, so there's room for a conversation.

If you have 90 minutes, you could have a 45-minute three-person panel based on this format with room for several follow-up questions, plus a 30-minute Q&A or 30-minute small group discussion in facilitated breakout rooms.

Why is this better than each panelist answering every question? From the participants' perspective, it's much more engaging to see interaction and conversation among panelists than to see each simply recite their own perspectives, devoid of any response to what others said. From the panelists' perspective, it's a lot easier to prep for a panel when you're told you'll have one primary and one secondary question, which you'll know in advance. It's also great to be aware of what other panelists might be talking about and how their expertise relates to this topic.

Benefits of Modular Design

In a 90-minute program, it's possible to include more than one of these formats and/or a breakout room segment. Thinking about your session in segments and knowing which segments support which outcomes will help you make decisions on the fly if you need to shorten your program unexpectedly or if your participants need additional time in one of the segments.

Determining which segments are critical for the outcomes you've selected will also help you trim down your content ahead of time. I know this can be difficult. You're an expert and have so much knowledge to share. But too much information is actually not helpful. It's the law of diminishing returns. More content leads to less retention, and too many possible next steps lead to inaction.

The good news is that you can share additional content with participants in a few ways, including:

- Skip some slides during the session but keep them in the PDF of the slides you share.

- Provide a handout with additional information.

- Create a "lead magnet" on your website. This is a web link that requires participants to opt-in to your email list to receive additional information.

- Offer a follow-up program that goes into depth about your topic.

- Direct participants to your YouTube channel to watch video tutorials.

Having fun yet? So many interesting ways to design a session. And yes, these strategies work for in-person and virtual events. There are some additional considerations when designing for an in-person experience—mainly around creating a welcoming and inclusive space for those who are overwhelmed with navigating those vibrant, chaotic hallways. I'd love to support your in-person or virtual event by providing strategic event design to help you achieve specific objectives for your participants. Reach out, and we can schedule a Speaker Strategy Session. Email action@BreakOutofBoredom.com.

CHAPTER FIVE

Engagement Tools

To keep things interesting for participants, weave in interactive tools during your 60, 75, or 90-minute virtual session. Practice using the tools ahead of time, so you're comfortable with any you choose. The first time you try a new tool should *not* be in front of an audience. Invite a few friends to join you for a practice call where you can test out a tool and get their feedback from a participant's perspective.

In this chapter, I share examples of how I use certain features (such as closing the waiting room and admitting all participants) that I explained in detail in other chapters. For example, Chapter Three has a section on waiting rooms. If you're unsure how to use one of the features I mention in this chapter, look in the Table of Contents for the section where I explain it in detail.

WELCOME BOX

My first engagement tool suggestion happens pre-event. A welcome box is a wonderful way to set the tone that your event will not be a typical boring webinar. This is also an opportunity to highlight sponsors. You could even make the case that a branded item in a welcome box will get more visibility than something picked up at an exhibitor booth at a conference. I often leave swag in my hotel room, rather than pack it all in my suitcase. In contrast, swag in welcome boxes I've received for virtual events has stayed on or near my desk for months.

What should you put into your welcome box?

Paper emojis (with or without a stick)—Invite participants to hold one of these (a heart, laughing emoji, or thumbs up) in front of their camera instead of clicking on the **Reactions** button to select an emoji. You could brand these emojis using your event colors. Last-minute registrants could print these out at home.

Do Not Disturb sign—Are participants joining from home where they might be disturbed by a partner or children? In 2020, I produced the first-ever virtual HomeDadCon for The National At-Home Dad Network.[1] Held annually, this virtual event for stay-at-home dads was renamed DadCon@Home. Their welcome box included door tags that could be used after the event: *"DO NOT DISTURB Go Find The Other (Responsible) Adult At Home!"*

FIGURE 5.1. Branded door tag that participants use year-round.

Whiteboard and marker—This was just one of the clever items shipped by one of my clients, Notary Symposium.[2] The small board was in the shape of a word cloud. During the event, speakers invited participants to write one or two words on the board and hold it up to the camera. (As I mentioned in *The Future is Left - Mirroring Online* section in the *Online Facilitation* chapter, the text will always look correct for participants even if it looks backwards on your screen because you're mirroring.)

Lightbulb image—Another idea from the Notary Symposium. Participants were asked to hold up an image with a lightbulb and the word "THIS!" at the top to share that they were having a "lightbulb moment." This is a fun way to find out what content is resonating with participants. The top of the back said, "Are you writing it down?" and on the bottom were instructions from a sponsor, Get Known Strategy,[3] on how to access free content that will help participants create a year's worth of social media posts. A great way to get sponsor branding in front of participants.

FIGURE 5.2. An example of an inexpensive, clever way to get participants to interact with your brand and hold onto your promotional material beyond the event.

Tea, candle, sweet treat, sticky notes, and markers—These were some of the items shipped ahead of an event I attended hosted by Sensible Woo.[4] A few weeks before the event, I was asked to complete a short survey about my likes. My future self was quite pleased by my past self's selections, which I had initially forgotten

I'd even made. Each item was exactly what I liked. This level of personalization was possible because it wasn't a large event. If it had been bigger, creating a selection of packages to choose from (such as sweet, salty, and savory or vanilla, chocolate, and strawberry) would allow attendees a choice.

While you can purchase, package, and ship everything on your own, there are fulfillment centers that will do this for large-scale events. Google *"fulfillment center virtual event welcome box"* to find companies that provide this service. While it's an added expense, consider how much you're saving by not paying for coffee, snacks, meals, room rentals, security, lodging, planes, mileage. . . you get the picture. While a virtual event will be less expensive than an in-person event, that doesn't mean you should not have a budget. The Welcome Box is an opportunity to highlight sponsors and it's also something a sponsor could underwrite for greater visibility.

Does it have to be a physical box?

Uber Eats vouchers[5]—At the end of 2022, Zoom invited me to a free invite-only event to learn about updates coming in 2023. While I wanted to hear this information, the timing didn't fit well into my schedule. I registered, marked my calendar, and debated whether to rearrange my schedule to attend live or plan to watch the replay. The day before, I opened an email from Zoom letting me know that I would be receiving a $25 Uber Eats voucher for lunch that would only be valid for the day of the event. That was all the encouragement I needed. I attended live. It turned out I was one of only four participants with a camera on, which meant I was able to ask several questions directly to the speakers.

KNOW BEFORE YOU GO

Want to increase attendance? Make it easy for participants to find the Zoom link when they're ready to join your meeting. The Uber Eats voucher I just mentioned was sent by Zoom in an email that included "Know Before You Go" in the subject line. The email explained that a confirmation email with my personalized Zoom link had been sent after completing the registration form. An email like this is also helpful if you've collected RSVPs through another process and want to send out a last-minute reminder of how to join the Zoom meeting and what to expect.

If you set up a Zoom meeting registration page, you have the option to manually resend the confirmation email.[6] As I mention in the *Scheduling a Meeting* section of the *Settings* chapter, I recommend editing the subject line of this email to be "[Meeting Topic] ZOOM LINK"—rather than "[Meeting Topic] Confirmation" which is the default subject line. You can also edit the text of this email to include additional "know before you go" information, such as:

- Agenda, specifically the timing of breaks
- A request to come camera-ready and without background noise to be able to more fully participate in breakout rooms
- Advance reading materials reminder
- Slide deck to review in advance
- Update Zoom reminder

Include anything that will help participants prepare for and benefit from the experience.

To resend the Zoom meeting confirmation email:

1. Log into www.Zoom.us.

2. Click on **Meetings** on the left menu.

3. Select your meeting.

4. Click on **Registration**.

5. Click on **View**.

6. ✓ box on the top left to select all registrants on that page.

7. Click **Resend Confirmation Email** button.

8. Scroll down to advance to the next page.

9. Repeat steps 6-8 until you've reached the last page.

Using Zoom webinar registration?
When you set up your webinar, in addition to the confirmation email, you can choose whether to schedule a reminder email for one hour, one day, and/or one week before the webinar start time. A follow-up email can be sent one to seven days after to attendees and absentees (those who registered but didn't attend).[7]

MUSIC

Early in 2020, I set myself apart by opening each Zoom event I hosted with a burst of upbeat music. It often meant that within a few minutes of the meeting starting someone would ask in chat, "How do you play music in Zoom?"

The answer:

1. You need to be the host or co-host of a meeting (or the meeting settings allow participants to share their screen).

2. Look at the bottom middle of your Zoom window and click on the **Share Screen button** on the toolbar.

3. Then click on the word **Advanced** at the top of the white pop-up window.

4. Then click on **Computer Audio** on the next screen.

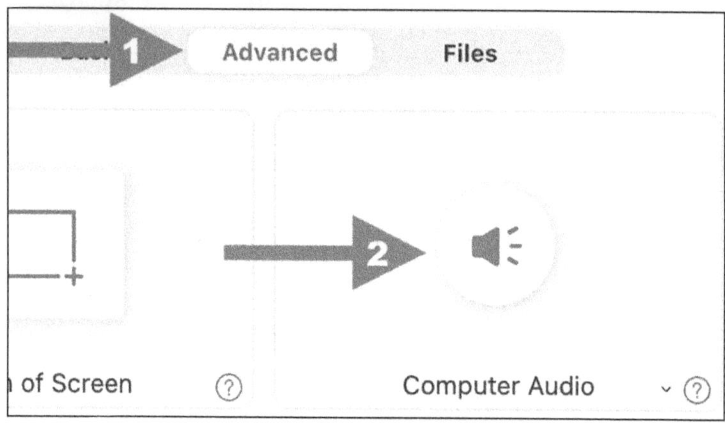

FIGURE 5.3. After clicking the green **Share Screen** button on the bottom of the Zoom window, click **Advanced** at the top of the pop-up window and then **Computer Audio**.

Now, Zoom will play any sound it hears on your computer—so turn off all your app notifications that bing before playing music from iTunes, Pandora, Amazon Music, Spotify, YouTube, or a file on your computer.

Looking for royalty-free music?
Search "royalty-free" on YouTube, Spotify, or Amazon Music. You'll find something that will work with any event.

Asking *how* to play music is a fine question, but the better question is *why* do I play music in Zoom?

Let me paint a picture. This is your first time attending this Zoom event, and you join the call two minutes before the official start time. There's no waiting room. You are immediately placed in the main room, where you notice a handful of people already there who are deep into conversation. For a moment, you wonder to yourself, "Am I late? Did I get the timing wrong?"

As a participant, this can be disconcerting. You think you're on time, even a minute or two early, but the host is deep into a sidebar conversation with a few participants. It's not a topic you know anything about, so you and the other 30+ participants join the meeting and sit quietly, wondering what you're missing or whether you got the time or topic wrong.

Another possibility. You are the host of the meeting. You let in a few people who arrived early or didn't have a waiting room enabled. The first three people to join immediately get into a discussion, while another 30 participants trickle in over the next few minutes. It's now time to start the meeting, but these three participants are not getting the hint. They keep going. They're starting to wrap up their conversation but not doing so very quickly. You're now left in the awkward position of trying to figure out how to step in and politely wrestle the microphone back—while the rest of the room watches. You'll have to be super direct rather than subtle to shut down the sidebar chat. It's not a smooth "curtains open" experience.

I use a combination of music and waiting rooms to create the social cues I believe we all need to have in this virtual environment.

Waiting rooms are key. At first, I wasn't using waiting rooms for my weekly #NoMoreBadZoom Virtual Happy Hours.[8] I would arrive five minutes early to my Zoom room to get set up and find 12 people already in the room deep in conversation. I then tried showing up ten minutes early, but my community had been trained to show up early for an unofficial chat, and I found eight people already logged in and chatting.

I learned that if I wanted to control the participant experience, especially for first timers, I needed to be more thoughtful about how I opened each event.

These are the meeting settings I use:

- **Waiting room** enabled

- **Passcode** enabled

- **Mute participants upon entry**

When I'm ready, but no more than two minutes before the official start time, I start playing a song, then close the waiting room and admit all participants. When they come in, they're automatically muted, and they hear the music. If I'm producing an event for a client, I also add a slide with a countdown clock—see the *Countdown Clock* section below for how to set this up. This way, participants can confirm for themselves that they can see and hear everything, but I'm controlling how the event begins.

It's important not to break this social cue by speaking over the music. If a participant unmutes to say hello to me, I smile at them and give a quick wave, then mute them. If I respond, everyone will believe it's appropriate to speak over the music.

I usually begin the meeting one or two minutes after the official start time. I like to give participants a little grace, especially since many of us are zooming from one Zoom to another all day with nary a bio break to be seen.

While I'm staying muted, I'm still communicating with participants by writing a note in chat:

> *Welcome! We will begin in a few minutes. Please update your name to include your pronouns (if you'd like) and organization.*
>
> *On a Mac? Click on your own video and select **Rename**. On a PC? Right-click on your own video and select **Rename**. On a phone or iPad? Click **Participants** and then on your name.*
>
> *Meanwhile, enjoy the music.* ♪♪

Participants will only see chat messages posted while they're in the room, so this welcome message needs to be repeated every 30-60 seconds as participants join the call.

If there's no countdown clock slide, I might lower the volume of the music after a minute to let folks know we'll be getting started soon and invite them to read what I posted in chat, then the music is turned back up to the original volume.

What's the right volume?

Each music player (Pandora, Spotify, Amazon Music, etc.) has an adjustable volume. Record yourself playing music through Zoom at different levels. Listen to the recording to figure out what level is loud enough that it's clear that no one should be speaking over the music but not so loud that it will be jarring as participants join the meeting.

When the countdown clock runs out, or it's been a minute or two after the official start time, I turn off the music (and stop sharing if I had been sharing the countdown clock slide) and warmly welcome everyone while looking right at the camera.

If I'm recording the event with the intention of sharing the replay, I edit out the video while the music was playing, so the replay viewers don't have to wait for the event to begin.

> *By default, when breakout rooms close, there's an extra 60 seconds before everyone is automatically brought back to the main room. Before I knew there was an option to switch those 60 seconds to 15 seconds, I regularly played a minute of music while we waited for everyone to exit the breakout rooms.*

COUNTDOWN CLOCK

This isn't so much about interaction as it is about creating the best opening for your event. It eliminates those awkward moments just before a program begins when only a few people are unmuted and chatting away while everyone else is watching them like they're in a fishbowl.

Instead, I recommend creating a positive experience from the beginning and avoiding this social awkwardness. I want participants to know right away that they're in the correct place and can see and hear what's happening on the screen. This way, if they have technical issues, they can be resolved before the meeting is underway.

My best practice is to play a six-minute countdown clock that begins four minutes before the program's start time when I'm in the green room with the speaker(s) and the participants are still in the waiting room. This lets speakers know we're about to let participants into the main room. Places, everybody, places!

FIGURE 5.4. A mock-up of a branded countdown clock slide.[9]

As I start the countdown clock slide, I also start playing a song. I time the song (or two songs if they're short) to end when the clock reaches zero. The music is selected to help create a mood. If I'm hosting an event that's for a California-based organization and it's 8:30 am PT, I select a soothing instrumental or something else low-key. If it's 2 pm ET, I'll play something upbeat and catchy.

> *A colleague runs a speaker series for her department and has the presenters choose their intro and outro music to give the participants a view into the presenter's personality.*

I've learned not to put the first speaker into the spotlight next to the countdown clock slide as participants join the meeting, as they're often checking their notes, adjusting the setup on their desktop, and generally doing everything except looking at the camera.

Instead, I'll change my virtual background to a full screen image of their company logo, then cover my camera. Then I'll spotlight myself, but only the logo will be showing. To be clear, I'm *not* turning off my camera, I'm *covering* it. Getting a privacy cover for your webcam will make this simple. For many months, I was taping a business card over my camera, as that's what I had handy. Turns out the solution cost only $6 for 2 covers.[10]

Participants who were rushing in exactly on time from another Zoom call (we've all been there) see there's still two minutes on the countdown clock and have time to take care of any biological needs (bathroom, refresh water, let the dog out) without missing anything. Those who are not in a rush can settle in and say hello in chat. Often participants will comment on the music selection, especially if it's a multi-day conference that I'm producing and I play different music at the start of each session.

No one speaks over the music. This includes me and all of the speakers. As I mentioned earlier, speaking over the music breaks this social cue that's been set, and you're back to having sidebar conversations happening in front of everyone while they compete with the music's volume.

Participants are muted as they enter the main room, based on the setting I selected when scheduling the meeting. In the green room, I explain that I'll be playing music and muting all of the speakers as we let participants in. I let the first speaker know that I need them to unmute when there are 30 seconds left on the countdown clock, so I know they're ready and paying attention. If necessary, I'll click on the **Ask to Unmute** button on their video to get their attention. I also let them know that when there are 10 seconds left on the clock, I'll spotlight them, so look alert.

I confirm the speaker has unmuted at 30 seconds, put them in the spotlight at ten seconds, and then lower the volume on the music before stopping the screen share. That's the cue for the first speaker to welcome participants.

Depending on the event, this will be a quick hello before the first speaker turns the microphone over to me for a Zoom Participant Orientation and housekeeping, then back to the first speaker for their welcome remarks. The recording is edited to begin with these welcome remarks, removing the countdown clock, music, and my housekeeping remarks from the replay.

Now that I've explained the purpose of the countdown slides, you're probably wondering how to create them. While it's possible to insert a countdown clock into a PowerPoint slide, I don't recommend this option.[11] If you click outside of the PowerPoint program, perhaps to check your run of show, the clock stops counting down. Instead, I recommend using Google Slides for this purpose—even if you plan to use PowerPoint for the rest of your slides. You can click outside of Google Slides and the countdown clock will not be disrupted.

TO SET UP GOOGLE SLIDE COUNTDOWN CLOCK

1. Search and add the Slides Timer Chrome plug-in from the Chrome Web Store. [12]

2. Open this Google Slide and make a copy of the file: https://robbiesamuels.com/countdownclocktemplate

3. Follow these instructions:

   a. Create timers using placeholders (e.g., <<0:00+>>, <<5:00->>, <<time>>)

   b. Times placed between << and >> will be replaced with a timer.

   c. Use - as the last character to count *down* from the specified time. Use + to count *up* from the specified time. Use **<<time>>** to display the current time.

   Example:

   <<5:00->> will count down starting at 5 minutes.

   <<2:00+>> will count up starting at 2 minutes

   d. <<time>> will display the current time on your computer in AM/PM format.

When designing the slide, make sure you leave room for the timer text. This needs to be slightly to the right of where you want it to be when in presentation mode to line up correctly. It's trial and error to get this right.

Do you have more than one monitor? Move these slides to a second monitor, so they can be full screen when you share them.

Only have one monitor? Adjust the window where the Google Slides play so it only takes up a portion of your screen when it's in presentation mode. See the steps in the next sidebar.

PRESENTING GOOGLE SLIDES COUNTDOWN SLIDE, USING ONLY A PORTION OF YOUR SCREEN:

1. Open the Google Slides countdown file. There must be no other tabs on that browser window, as all tabs will show if you're not playing the slide full screen.

2. *Do **NOT** press ESC to reduce from full screen.*

3. Click on the **Present** button.

4. Bring your cursor to the bottom left corner of the screen. The number of the slide will appear, along with arrows on either side and three vertical dots.

   a. Click the **three vertical dots.**

   b. Select **Exit Full Screen**.

5. If on a PC, reduce the entire window using the **Restore Down** button in the upper right-hand corner. This is not necessary on a Mac.

   a. *Do not minimize the window.* The entire tab must be visible on your computer screen for you to share on Zoom.

   b. Adjust the dimensions of the window to remove the black bars on the top/bottom or left/right, but don't make it too small, or the image will have poor resolution for participants. Half of the laptop screen is ok. To adjust dimensions, hover the cursor on the bottom left corner until you see a double-headed arrow as the cursor. Then, drag the window up and to the right to remove the black bars on the sides and top of the slide.

   c. Once you start the countdown clock, Zoom and other programs can overlap with the countdown slide (i.e., cover it).

FIGURE 5.5. When you exit full screen in Google Slides, you need to adjust the window's dimensions to remove the black bars. The same is true if you have one monitor and use PowerPoint's **Browsed by an individual (window)** option.[13]

I'm sharing detailed steps for the Google Slides Countdown Clock below, and you can also download all the steps and links as a PDF at www.robbiesamuels. com/breakout. That way, you'll have it readily available when you need to follow these steps one by one.

Steps to Sharing the Countdown Clock

1. Your Countdown Clock Google Slides should be open and ready to share (see above).

    a. Cue a song selection from your music source (such as Spotify, iTunes, Amazon Music).

    b. Copy the **Welcome** text that you would like to paste into **Chat** while participants are waiting for the session to start.

    c. **Mute** everyone in the **Main Room** except yourself.

2. Four minutes before show time, put your cursor on the first slide of the countdown clock deck and click to advance to the next slide, which starts the countdown clock.

3. Click **Record**.

4. Press the **Share** button on Zoom. On the **Basic tab, ✓ Share Sound** at the bottom and double-click on the **Countdown Clock Google Slides**.

5. Your Zoom toolbar is now floating at the TOP of your screen.

6. Start playing the music at a moderate volume. *Test this ahead of time, as it's different for every music source.*

7. Ask the presenters in the **Main Room**—who should all now be muted—to give a thumbs up if they see the Countdown Clock counting down AND hear the music.

8. If you haven't already, on the Zoom toolbar open the **Chat** and the **Participants** windows.

9. Mute yourself.

10. Select a virtual background (e.g., company logo)

11. Cover your camera.

12. Spotlight yourself.

13. At two minutes before show time, click on the **Security** button on the bottom of the Zoom window and then uncheck **Enable the Waiting Room** (this closes the waiting room).

14. At the top of the **Participants** window, click on **Admit All** (this let's in all participants from the waiting room).

15. For the next four minutes, paste the **Welcome** text into chat every 30 seconds.

16. Have the welcome speaker **Unmute** when there are 30 seconds left on the clock so you know they're paying attention.

17. When the clock has ten seconds left, **Replace Spotlight** the first speaker.

18. Then, lower the volume on the music to zero and click the red **Stop Share** button.

Yeah, that's a lot of steps. Yet another reason to hire a professional Zoom producer who can handle all the tech angst for you. Designing the opening is just the start (pun intended), but participants most remember how they felt at the beginning and the end of an event. Have you ever had to wait a long time for coat check or valet? That colored how you felt about that event. The same is true for virtual events. Design matters.

POLLS, ADVANCED POLLS, AND QUIZZES

Have you tried out **Advanced Polls** and **Quizzes**? So many more ways to creatively engage with participants. Before I get into that, let me remind you that polls are only available for paid Zoom accounts (Pro, Business, or Enterprise). Also, polls may be connected to a specific meeting link, or you may add the poll to a **Central Library** (this option needs to be enabled by the account administrator).[14]

Polls

Let's get started with how to add a basic poll to a specific meeting:[15]

- Schedule a meeting at <u>www.Zoom.us</u> and hit save. Then scroll to the top of the screen and click on **Polls.**

- Click the **Create** button.

- Name the poll.

- What is the question or prompt?

- What are the answers (up to 10)?

- Can participants select just one (**Single Choice**) or more than one answer (**Multiple Choice**)?

Something to consider: Do you want to have more than one question in your poll or multiple polls? If you **Add a Question,** you'll have one poll with two (or more) questions. Every question needs to be answered before participants can submit their answers. Instruct participants to scroll down on the right side to view the next question; when they've answered all the questions, they will be able to hit submit. Co-hosts should be told in the green room not to touch the poll as they cannot answer it and could accidentally close it (it's happened to me!)

*I recommend closing the poll when at least 70% of participants have responded or two minutes have passed—whichever comes first. Tell participants, "I'm going to end the poll in about 10 seconds. Finish up and hit the **Submit** button, so your responses are included. 5, 4, 3, 2, 1. OK. I'm closing the poll, now let's look at the results." Then click **Share Results** to discuss the responses with participants. Remember to stop sharing the results before moving on with your program.*

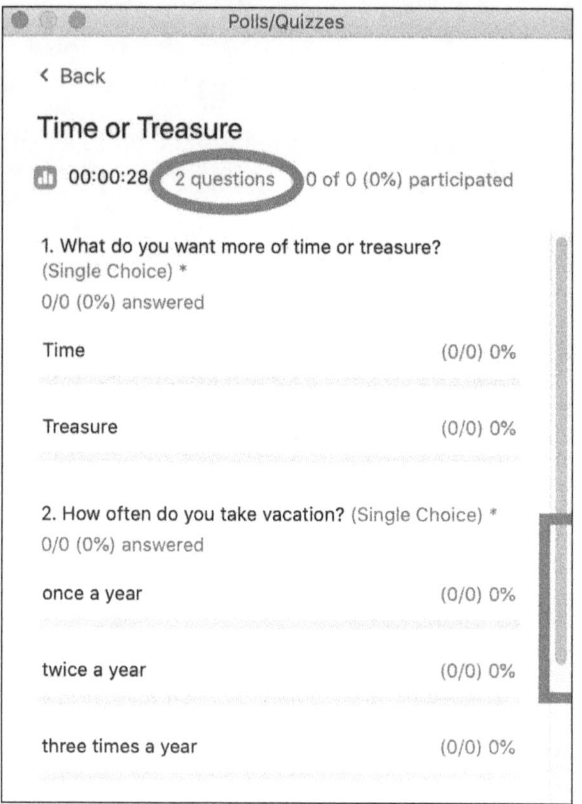

FIGURE 5.6. Remind participants to scroll down on the right side of the pop-up window to view and respond to all questions before hitting the submit button.

If the plan is to launch a poll at the start of your presentation and another at the end, that should be two separate polls. Each may have one or more questions, but you would need to create a second poll for the one being shared at the end of the meeting.

The order in which you add a poll is the order it will appear on the list when you click on **Polls** during the meeting. For this reason, it's helpful to finalize your run of show (agenda) before adding polls to the meeting. Also, name the poll something distinct that will help you know when to launch it.

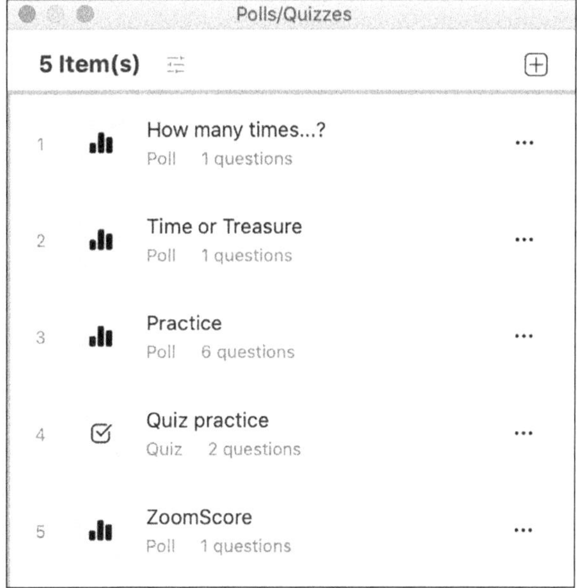

FIGURE 5.7 If you have more than one poll created for a meeting, it will appear in a list. Hover over a poll or quiz, and a **Launch** button will become visible.

What is your ZoomScore™?
Rosemary Ravinal created this 10-point checklist of the components of a professional video presence.[16]

If you want to ask the same question at the start and the end of the meeting—and want to see responses from both polls to compare percentages—create two polls instead of relaunching the first poll. Relaunching wipes out the initial responses and they're no longer available as a downloadable report.

Poll results can create breakout room assignments
Select this option as you set up the poll question.[17]

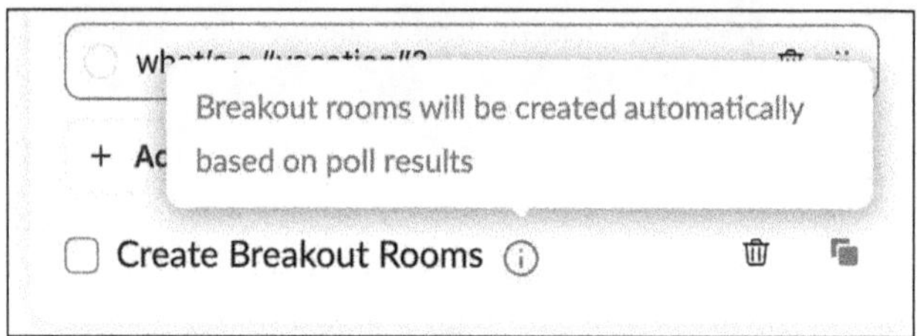

FIGURE 5.8. ✓ **Create Breakout Rooms** when you add the poll question.

Poll Templates

If you set up an intricate poll for a meeting that will be scheduled again, you have two choices. If the meeting recurs at a regular interval (weekly, every two weeks), schedule that meeting as a recurring meeting and the poll will be available every time. If the meeting occurs at irregular intervals, you can save the meeting as a template. The poll will then be available each time you select the template as you schedule a new meeting. Either option will save you from having to add the polls to a meeting link again.

Poll Central Library

This is an account-level setting that allows all users on that Zoom account to have up to 10 polls available across all their meetings.

If you're using a Pro Zoom account, you're the account administrator and can enable this feature. If you're a user who is part of a Business or

Enterprise Zoom account, you'll need to contact your account administrator to ask for this feature to be enabled.

- The account administrator logs in at <u>www.Zoom.us</u>.
- On the left menu, scroll down to click **Account Management**, then select **Account Settings**.
- Search for the word: **Polls** or click on **In Meeting** (Basic) to locate **Meeting Polls**.
- ✓ **Allow users to manage saved polls and quizzes from meeting**.
- **Save**.

Advanced Polls and Quizzes

What options are available with Advanced Poll? This is how Zoom describes this feature:[18]

- **Single Choice**: Poll participants can select only one of the provided answers. Possible answers can be listed all at once or under a drop-down menu.
- **Multiple Choice**: Poll participants can select more than one of the provided answers.
- **Matching**: Poll participants can match prompts on the left side with answers on the right side. Order of prompts and answers can be adjusted as needed. Up to nine prompts can be provided for each question, with the possible matches ranging between two to nine options.
- **Rank Order**: Poll participants can rank each item based on the provided scale. Up to ten items can be provided for each question, with the scale allowing a range of two to seven options.

- **Short Answer**: Poll participants can respond with a short answer response. The minimum and maximum allowed characters for the response can be set.

- **Long Answer**: Poll participants can respond with a long answer response. The minimum and maximum allowed characters for the response can be set.

- **Fill in the blank**: Poll participants are presented with the statement and a blank, asking them to fill in the missing information based on the statement and other context provided. Multiple blanks can be added and each blank has its own answer box.

- **Rating scale**: Poll participants are given a statement or topic, then are given the opportunity to rate the topic on a given scale. The range of the scale can be adjusted from the default of one to ten, and the ends of the scale can be labeled to indicate what the scale is based on, for example **Not likely** to **Extremely likely**.

Other options:

- **Make a quiz and set correct answers**

- **Add to Polls/Quizzes library**: Your created poll will be saved to a poll/quiz library, where you can access and reuse your poll again for future meetings. This is only available if your account settings allow a **Central Library** for polls.

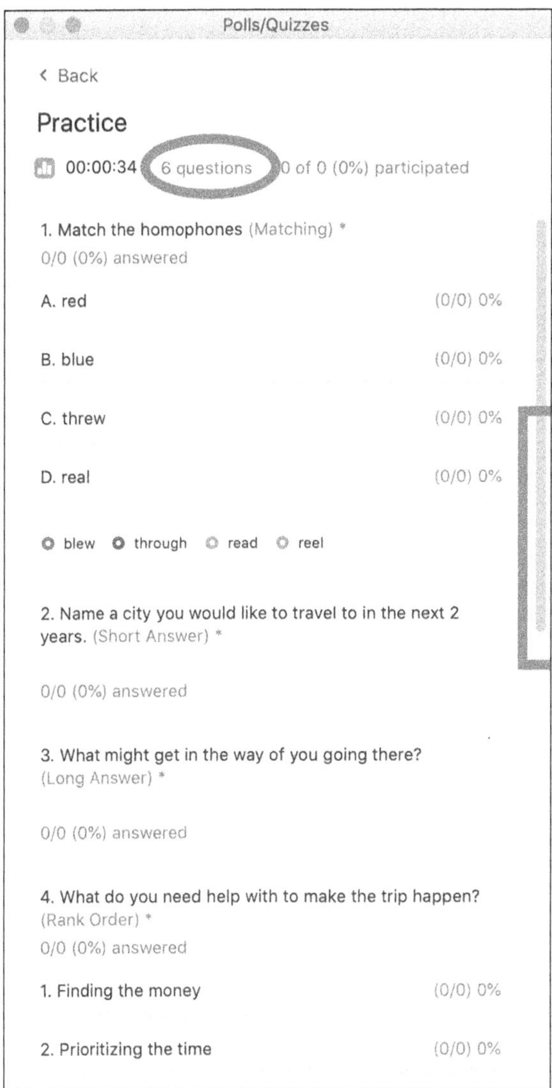

FIGURE 5.9. Example of **Advance Poll** questions and the need to scroll down on the right to respond to all the questions before hitting the submit button.

Creating a poll that allows participants to type in their answer was particularly exciting for me, because I could see so many potential scenarios where that would be useful. Even so, when **Advanced Polls and Quizzes** became available in late 2021, I wasn't immediately advocating its use, because participants who did not have Zoom version 5.8.3 weren't able to see or participate in the advanced polls or quizzes. Participants using company-issued laptops often have issues updating their Zoom Desktop Client (a.k.a. the computer app).

In November 2022, all Zoom users were required to update to a minimum Zoom version 5.8.6, so this is no longer a concern. As I mention in the section on updating Zoom in the *Settings* chapter, there's now a quarterly minimum update requirement. For example, as of February 4, 2023, all Zoom users were required to update to 5.10.3.

How do you set up Advanced Polls?

If you have a Pro account you can enable the **Advanced Poll and Quizzes** option while in **Account Settings**, while enabling the **Central Library** for polls. Anyone with a paid account can enable these options at the user-level **Zoom.us** Settings.

- Log into www.Zoom.us.

- On the left menu, click on **Settings.**

- Search for the word: **Polls** or click on **In Meeting** (Basic) to locate **Polls.**

- Enable **Meeting Polls/Quizzes**.

- Select any or all of the following:

  - Allow host to create advanced polls and quizzes.

  - Allow host to upload image for each question.

  - Allow alternative host to add or edit polls and quizzes.

  - Require answers to be anonymous.

- **Save**

View and Download Poll Responses

In most scenarios, it's important that you share the poll results with participants. To do so:

- Click **End Poll.**

- Click **Share Results.**

Another option is to click on the **three dots (. . .)** to select **View Results from Browser**, which will display the same percentages in a web browser.

Set up a Quiz and show correct answers

After ending the poll and sharing the results, ✓ the **Show correct answers to all** box.

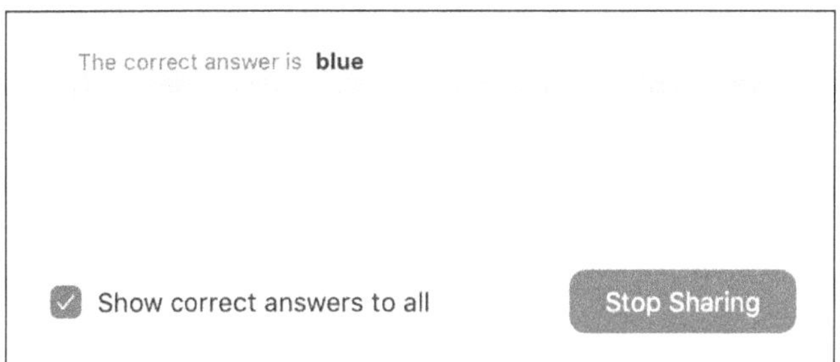

FIGURE 5.10. The correct answer to a **Quiz** question can be shown to all participants.

If you want to quickly access how each participant responded, there's a feature called **Download** results, which shares individual poll responses in a web browser.

If you do not have this feature, you can request it via Zoom Support: https://support.zoom.us/hc/en-us/requests/new or ask the ChatBot on the bottom right corner of www.Zoom.us.

Recording to the cloud? There's a cloud recording setting: **Save poll results shared during the meeting/webinar.**

Poll Reports

And lastly, there's always the option to download a **Poll Report**, either within the meeting after the poll has ended, or after the meeting:

1. Log into **www.Zoom.us**.

2. On the left menu, click on **Reports**.

3. Select **Meeting**.

4. Adjust the date range and switch the drop-down to **Poll Report**.

5. **Search**.

6. Locate the correct meeting from the list and select **Generate**.

7. The report will process for a moment, and then a **Download** button will appear.

8. Download the report to your computer.

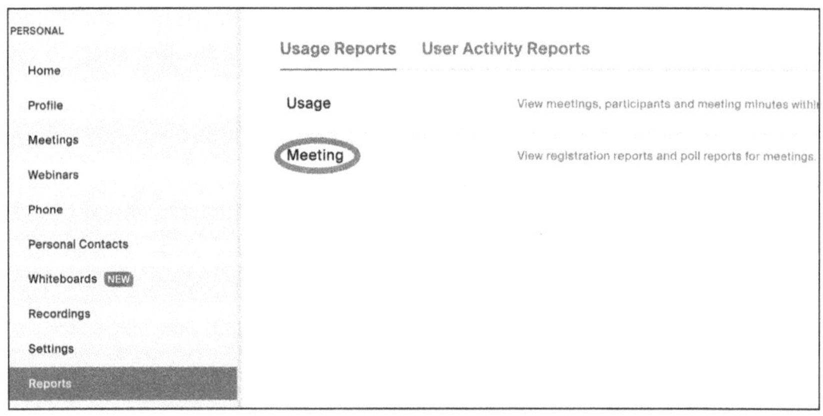

FIGURE 5.11. After logging into **Zoom.us**, click on **Reports** and then **Meeting** to locate the **Poll Reports**. This is the same location where you download registration reports, which I explain later in this section.

This will be a spreadsheet listing each participant's responses. It will not include the percentages that were visible when you shared results with participants during the meeting.

NON-VERBAL FEEDBACK (YES/NO)

If the question you want to ask participants has a binary answer (yes/no or true/false), then a poll isn't necessary.

Instead, use the **Non-Verbal Feedback** feature, which is located under the **Reactions** button on the bottom of the Zoom window.[19] The green check mark = yes and the red x = no, but you can always assign other meanings. For example, you can make the green check mark = true and the red x = false.

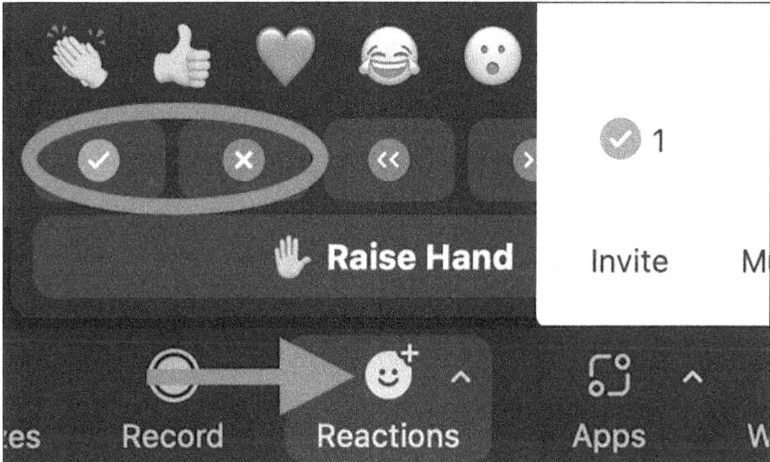

FIGURE 5.12. Direct participants to click the **Reactions** button and select either the green checkmark or the red X. Then open the **Participants** window to view results.

As participants select, view the tally in real-time at the bottom of the **Participant** window. This allows you to ask a spur-of-the-moment binary question and get immediate results. Ask, "Should we take a break now or after the next section?" and find out how participants are feeling.

Unlike emojis, the green check mark and red x will remain visible on each participant's video until they check that option a second time or the feedback is removed by a host or co-host.

To remove this feedback:

- Open **Participant** window.

- Click on **More** button on the bottom right.

- Click on **Clear All Feedback.**

Caution: This will also clear all raised hands. Design your run of show (agenda) so this question is not during a time when you've asked participants to raise their hands.

ANNOTATION

This feature allows the person sharing their screen and participants, if permitted, to draw on a slide, PDF, or the Zoom Whiteboard. To access, participants select View Options from the top of the Zoom window and then choose Annotate. A toolbar will appear with annotating options (e.g., text, draw, arrow, stamp).[20]

It can be a wonderfully collaborative tool, but it does have a bit of a learning curve. In my experience, the first time participants are given the option to use Annotation, they need a few minutes to play with all the features before settling down. They're so excited to be drawing and stamping, they remind me of three-year-olds with markers!

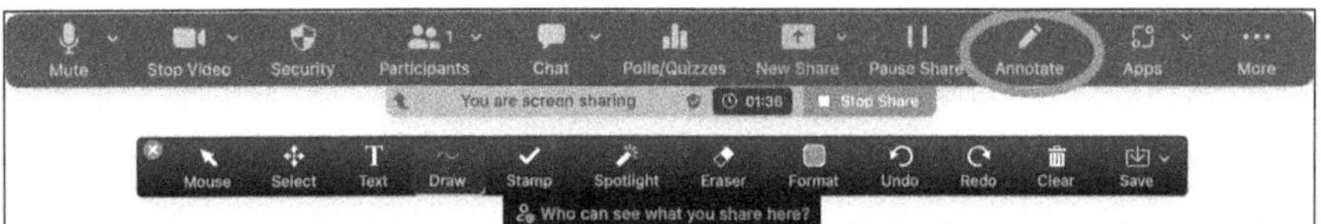

FIGURE 5.13. While sharing your screen, click the **Annotate** button on the floating toolbar to open the annotation tools. Test it out for yourself by clicking on these options.

I participated in one session where the speaker gave participants a practice slide before switching to the exercise on the next slide. This was a great idea, in theory, but one of the participants began to use the heart stamp to stamp a meta-heart, meaning a bigger heart made of smaller hearts. The meeting paused while we watched this participant finish their heart before the speaker moved to the exercise slide.

FIGURE 5.14. A participant used the heart stamp to make a mega-heart while we watched and waited.

For this reason, I tend to avoid using group annotation during a one-time 60 or even 75 minute virtual session, as there are often several other ways to get the same information from participants with less time.

During one of my speaker prep meetings, a speaker shared her plan to have participants use a stamp (one of the annotation tools) to select which three of 10 topics they wanted to explore more deeply during her presentation. Knowing how out-of-hand that could get and that she only had 75 minutes for her session, I recommended that she use a poll instead. All she needed to do was create a poll with 10 answers and tell participants to choose their top three. With the new **Advanced Polls**, she could now even ask them to rank their top three, so she would know precisely which topics were of greatest concern for her participants.

USING THIRD-PARTY TOOLS

With the introduction of Zoom Apps (a.k.a. Zapps)[21] and the Zoom App Marketplace,[22] Zoom has made it easier to integrate third-party tools (such as Miro, Mural, Mentimeter, Jamboard) into your meeting. Some of the Zapps, like a timer that appears on your screen, don't need your participants to do anything on their end. Others require participants to access a program outside of Zoom.

Before you decide to incorporate one of these tools into your event design, it's important to know how comfortable your participants will be using it. If you're meeting with them weekly throughout a semester or for a team meeting, then it makes more sense to spend time getting them used to one of these tools that will be used during each weekly meeting. On the other hand, if you have a limited amount of time with this group during an annual conference session, I recommend sticking with Zoom's built-in features.

Early in the pandemic, some participants clicked a link in chat, lost the Zoom window, and did not know how to get it back. What happened is they had their Zoom window full screen, so when they clicked on a link, the browser window replaced the Zoom window. Participants did not know how to quickly switch back to Zoom. The result was they're wary of clicking links in chat even now—three years later.

I share this because speakers often think that by providing a link to an app like Mentimeter or Mural, in chat, they're giving participants easy access to that resource. Talk to the meeting planner or organization liaison ahead of time to ask about this community's experience with the tool you plan to use. It may be one they have used frequently through this association or through the organization's own team meetings. This will also depend on how generally tech savvy an audience is, which often (but not always) correlates with the age of the audience.

One way to test the comfort of a group is to pay attention to what percentage participate using different tools. In my experience, a basic poll in Zoom will have 70-90% participation, while a Mentimeter poll may have only 50% participation. If high participation is your goal, incorporate Zoom's built-in engagement tools. With the **Advanced Poll** features, there are many new ways to engage participants and collect their feedback.

SECOND CAMERA

While you could purchase an external camera to use as a second camera, your mobile phone's camera would work just as well. Combine your mobile phone with a phone tripod to create a different angle to spotlight you, or to focus on what you're writing/drawing/building on your desk with the camera right above your hands.[23]

Just log in with a second device to have access to a second camera.

> *Caution: Do not log in as the host on both devices—or your polls will stop working. Log out of Zoom on the second device, so you're joining as a guest and not connected to the host Zoom account.*

SHARE IPHONE OR IPAD TO ZOOM

Another sharing option is to connect an iPhone or iPad to Zoom via AirPlay or a wired connection.[24] Why? Here are two examples where this would be useful: To show off an app your organization has created or to use a stylus to draw on an iPad.

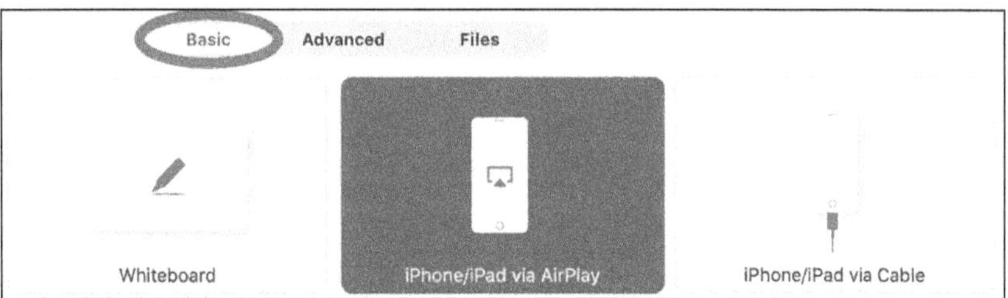

FIGURE 5.15. Click on the green **Share Screen** button at the bottom of the Zoom window and then select one of the two iPhone/iPad options.

- Join a Zoom meeting
- Click **Share Screen**
- Choose
  - iPhone/iPad via AirPlay

- – Share **sound** (optional)

- – Click **Share**

- On your iOS device's control center select **Screen Mirroring**

- Select **Zoom-your computer**

Or

- – iPhone/iPad via Cable

- – Share **computer sound** (optional)

- – Click **Share**

- – Connect via cable

- – Select **Trust**

- – Enter passcode if required

WHEEL OF NAMES

Who doesn't love to win? Use this interactive tool to encourage participants to register in advance, to give away sponsor gifts, or to select who will get the hot seat in your coaching session. Whatever your reason for wanting to pull a name out of a hat, this digital prize wheel is easily modified to fit your branding, theme, or just to be wildly colorful. It's also free and easy to hide the ads. www.wheelofnames.com

Adjust spin time
If you're going to use this tool to choose several names in a row, I recommend adjusting the **Spin Time** under the **Customize** menu.

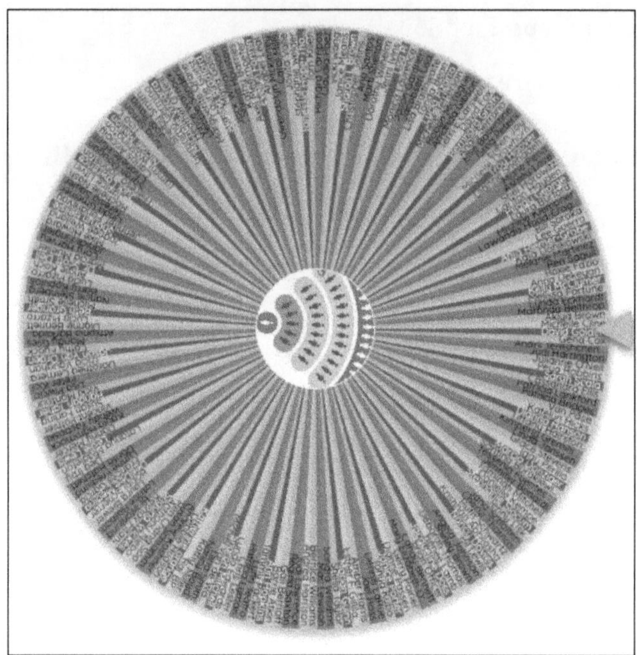

FIGURE 5.16. Example of a branded Wheel of Names. This one was used to give away prizes during the launch party for my second book, *Small List, Big Results: Launch a Successful Offer No Matter the Size of Your List.*[25]

POST-EVENT

Engagement doesn't have to end when you end the Zoom meeting. If you have a Pro, Business, or Enterprise Zoom account, you can run reports to find out who registered, who attended, and how participants responded to poll questions.[26] You can use this information to send *"Thanks for attending"* and *"Sorry we missed you"* emails.

*Knowing the poll results can help you personalize your follow-up message to offer additional resources or invite a participant to another event based on how they responded. See the Polls section in this chapter for details on how to download **Poll Reports.***

How to run reports:

- Log into www.Zoom.us (must be an account owner or have admin permissions)
  - On the left menu, select one of the following:
  - Click on **Reports** (listed below **Settings**).
- If that is not listed, click **Account Management > Reports**.
- **Meeting Registration Report** (aka RSVP list)

  The report may not be available for up to 30 minutes after a Zoom meeting.

  On the Usage Reports tab,
  - Select **Meeting**
  - Adjust dates
  - Dropdown: **Registration Report**
  - Click **Search** button
  - Locate meeting
  - Click **Generate** button
  - **All Registrants**
  - Click **Continue** button
  - Click **Download**

FIGURE 5.17. The attendance list is available under **Usage**. Registration list and poll results are available under **Meeting**.

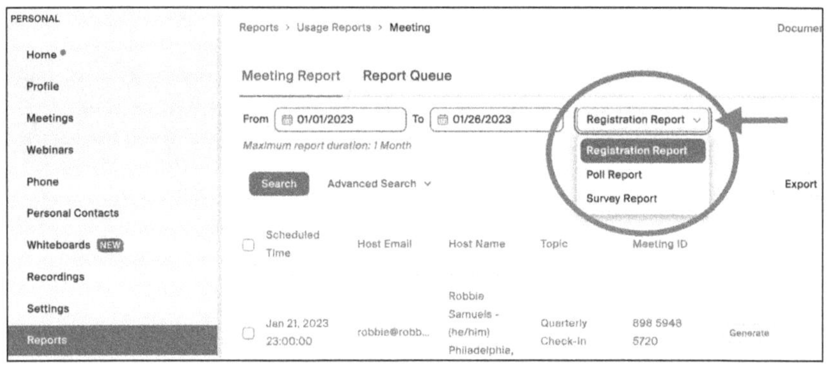

FIGURE 5.18. Remember to select **Poll Report** from the drop-down menu to download poll results.

- **Meeting Participants** (a.k.a. the attendance list)

  The report may not be available for up to 30 minutes after a Zoom meeting.

On the Usage Reports tab

- Select **Usage**

- Adjust dates

- Click **Search** button

- Locate meeting

- Scroll right to find the **Participants** column

- Click blue number

- ✓ **Export with meeting data** and **Show unique users** (on the top left)

- Click the **Export** button

Why can't you find a report?
This could be for a few reasons:

- Reports are only available for 12 months. If you may want this information, best to download it shortly after the meeting so you do not lose access.

- If a meeting is scheduled, but not started within 30 days of the scheduled date, Zoom may delete the meeting, which also deletes the Meeting Registration Report.

If the meeting was hosted by a free (Basic) Zoom account and later upgraded, the report will not become available.

Want to know what your participants thought of your meeting? Zoom also has a feature that will automatically send participants to a survey when they exit the meeting. This can be set up as either a Zoom poll or a third party survey website (SurveyMonkey, Typeform, or Jotform). If you don't see this option next to **Polls** on the Meeting page on Zoom. us, you will need to enable the **Meeting Survey** option discussed in the *Settings* chapter.

> *While it's technically possible to send participants to any link (such as your website), it may cause confusion if they click to respond to a survey and end up on your website. At this time, it's not possible to edit the text on the Zoom pop-up screen as participants exit the meeting.*

Beyond email, how might you stay in touch after the meeting? I hosted a full-day workshop. Afterward, I sent each participant a cube timer to help them set aside time to work on the strategies they'd learned.[27] Is there a book you want to send? A small poster? Whatever you send will be unexpected and make your event even more memorable.

Use a mix of these engagement tools throughout your 60, 75, or 90-minute virtual session to create an interactive and fun program. If you're unsure how to use some of the features I mentioned, check the Table of Contents to find the section of this book where I share that feature in detail.

CHAPTER SIX

Breakout Rooms

You know how I'm always talking about purpose-first design? Well, one of my main objectives for writing this book is to improve how breakout rooms are designed and facilitated. In fact, when it came time to write this book, I started by writing this chapter, because there are so many nuanced ways to create a stellar experience for participants when using breakout rooms. Unfortunately, too often, these techniques are not part of the virtual event design, but that's easy to fix once you know what's in this chapter.

I'd love to jump right into the second section, *What is the Purpose of the Breakout Room*, but before making a delicious meal, you need to confirm you have all the ingredients. For that reason, we start with *How to Set Up Breakout Rooms*. I'll explain the breakout room options that are key to providing your participants with a quality breakout room experience and what features aren't available in a breakout room.

We'll start with the basics and build from there. Ready? Let's go!

HOW TO SET UP BREAKOUT ROOMS

Co-hosts can set up and manage breakout room
If you're the host, your co-host can set up the breakout rooms while you're presenting. When the co-host opens the rooms, you won't be assigned to one, because hosts are never assigned to breakout rooms. That co-host also won't be assigned, because they're the ones who opened the breakout rooms.

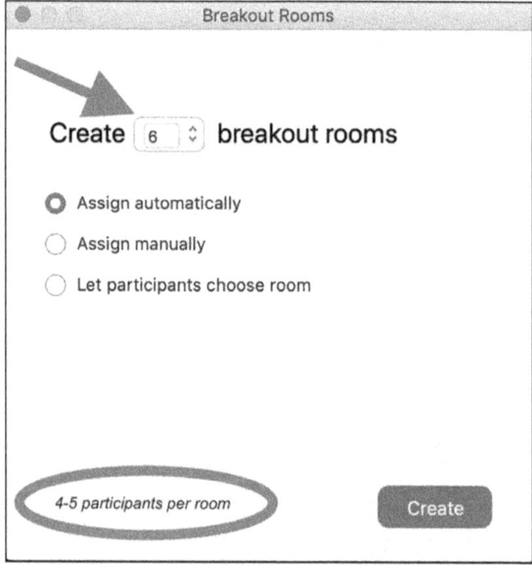

FIGURE 6.1. After clicking on the **Breakout Rooms** button, adjust the number of rooms and select the room style, then click the **Create** button.

Here's what you need to know to make the breakout room setup simple.[1]

Decide ahead of time how many participants per room and how long the breakout room will be open. This should be based on the purpose of the breakout room. See below for four examples.

After joining a Zoom meeting, click on the **Breakout Rooms** button at the bottom of the Zoom window (if your window is narrow, it may be hiding under the **More** button).

Adjust the number of rooms until the number of participants you planned per room is the number at the bottom of the pop-up window.

Choose the style of room (see *What Style of Breakout Room Works Best?* section below):

- Assign automatically (randomly).

- Assign manually (specific assignments).

- Let participants choose room.

- Click on the **Create** button.

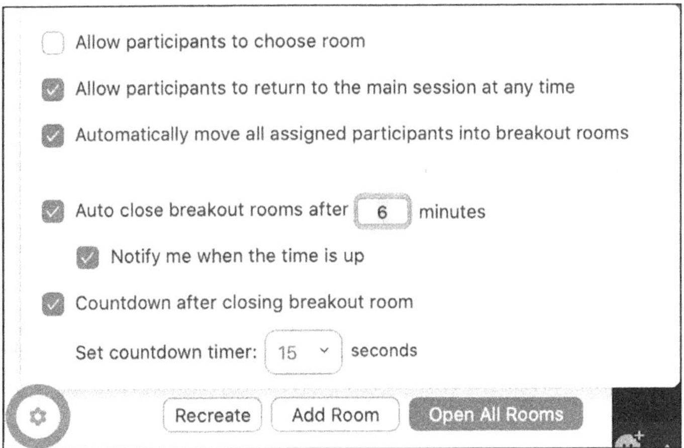

FIGURE 6.2. Before opening breakout rooms, adjust the options by clicking on the gear icon on the bottom left corner of the window.

On the next screen, click on the gear icon on the bottom left to adjust breakout room options.

- Allow participants to choose room
  - Leave unchecked if you selected **Assign Automatically** or **Assign Manually**.
  - This will automatically be checked if you selected **Let participants choose room** as your room style.
- Allow participants to return to the main session at any time.
  - When this box is checked, participants needing assistance do not need to leave the meeting and rejoin to the main room.
- Automatically move all assigned participants into breakout room.
  - When this box is checked, participants are sent to their assigned room as soon as you open the rooms.
  - Leave this unchecked if you want participants to click the pop-up button to join their assigned rooms (this may delay participants joining and is not recommended).
- Auto close breakout rooms after __ minutes
  - When this box is checked and the number of minutes added, a small countdown clock will appear on the top right in the breakout rooms showing how much time is remaining. This helps participants and facilitators keep track of time, so they aren't caught off guard when the breakout room closes.
- Notify me when the time is up.
  - When this box is checked, a pop-up will appear when the clock reaches zero. You will need to click a button to initiate a countdown timer.

- Leave it unchecked, and the countdown timer will initiate when the clock reaches zero.

- Set countdown timer: __ seconds

  - The default is 60 seconds. I recommend changing it to 15 seconds if you specified how many minutes the rooms will remain open.

Have you heard of the term "walkward"? It's when you say goodbye to someone while leaving a restaurant— only to walk in the same direction to find your parked cars. That same experience happens when the countdown clock in the breakout room counts down to 0:00 and participants are saying goodbye, only to have 60 seconds appear on the countdown timer. Some participants leave the room immediately, while others stick around, trying to decide whether 60 seconds is enough time for another comment. It's . . . awkward. Avoid that by changing the countdown timer to 15 seconds. That should be enough time for someone to finish their comment before rooms close and everyone is back in the main room.

WHAT FEATURES ARE NOT AVAILABLE IN BREAKOUTS?

Some features will not be available to participants in a breakout room, and others will only be available if the host enables it before the breakout rooms open.

Here's what's not possible in breakout rooms: spotlight, polls, captions, sign language interpretation, and language interpretation.

The ability to chat or share screen will match what's allowed in the main room. If direct messaging or sharing screen is disabled in the main room, it won't work in breakout rooms either. If you want to enable a setting for breakout rooms, enable it in the main room right before opening breakout rooms.

No matter the main room setting, participants can unmute in breakout rooms.

Cloud recording does not record breakout rooms, even if the host is in the room. Recording to the computer will record whatever room in which a host is located. A participant can be given permission to record a breakout room, but must have this permission before the breakout rooms open. (See the **Recording Options & Settings** section of the **Settings** chapter for more on this topic.)

Anything typed into the main room chat while participants are in breakout rooms will not be seen by participants. Messages typed into chat in a breakout room will only be visible to participants who are in the room when it was posted.

Co-hosts can record and share their screen in breakout rooms even if participants cannot. Remember to make facilitators co-hosts if you need them to share their screen.

WHAT IS THE PURPOSE OF THE BREAKOUT ROOM?

Now that you know the basics of setting up breakout rooms, let's discuss four reasons you would consider adding a breakout room to your agenda: as an icebreaker, to share insights, for discussion, and for a deep dive into a particular topic.

Remember, purpose-first design is based on being clear about the session's objectives, then using features and exercises that will help participants achieve those objectives. Breakout rooms often play a key role if peer-to-peer conversations or facilitator-led discussions would help participants understand the concepts shared during the content portion of the session.

I'll provide a description for each category, suggestions for the setup (i.e., the number of minutes and the number of participants per room), and an example.

Icebreaker

This is a brief activity that gives participants a chance to meet one or two fellow participants.

Setup: Two participants for five minutes, or three participants for six minutes.

If three participants are assigned to a room, there's a much lower likelihood that two of the three will have internet issues, so there's less of a chance that a participant will be left sitting on their own, wondering what happened. Also, three participants in a room gives every participant the chance to meet two other people instead of just one.

Example: Win/Win: This invites participants to share a personal and a professional win. This activity gives participants an opportunity to provide context for their professional connection to the group while also sharing something about their personal life, which may lead to stronger bonds with other group members.

> *If there are more than 10 rooms, I don't recommend two participants per room. It's difficult to keep an eye on all the pairs as rooms open. That means it's hard to determine whether any participants didn't connect to the breakout room, and if so, to make a quick adjustment, so the solo participant is not left alone for long.*

Share

This activity allows participants to share their answers to a prompt, but without extra time for discussion.

Setup: Four or five participants for 10 minutes

Example: "What's your biggest takeaway from the last presentation?" Each participant has about two minutes to share their answer, then it's time to go back to the main room.

Keep co-host(s) in the main room

Do you want to keep all speakers in the main room when the breakout rooms open? It used to be that you had to hunt through all the breakout rooms to unassign each speaker—a time-consuming endeavor. Now, if you make each speaker a co-host in the green room, you can uncheck Include **co-host(s) to breakout rooms** as you set up the breakout room. When the rooms open, speakers will stay in the main room. (This option will not appear if no one is a co-host.)

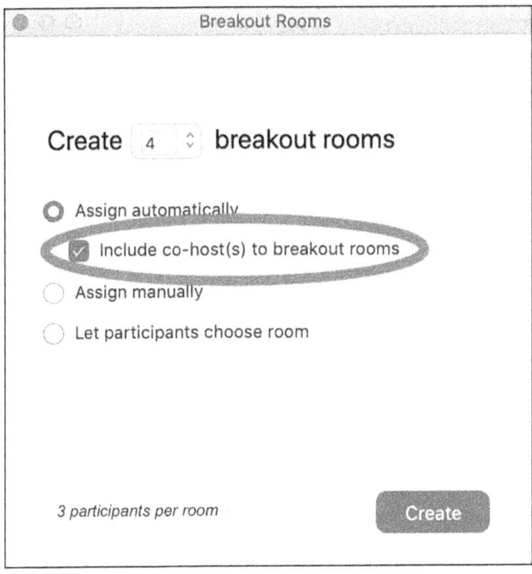

FIGURE 6.3. Zoom allows you to uncheck a box while setting up the breakout rooms, so co-hosts are not automatically assigned to a room.

Discussion

After each participant shares their answer to the prompt, there's time for a discussion inspired by the answers provided.

Setup: Up to six participants for up to 15 minutes.

Example: "If you had free time, what would you like to learn?" Each person takes up to two minutes to share their answer. In the time remaining, participants chat about what was shared and identify any common interests.

Deep Dive

Unlike the previous three examples, the purpose is not to have each participant share one after the other but to create space for a rich conversation.

Setup: Assigned facilitator (and optionally an assigned notetaker), with seven or more participants for 15+ minutes. Each facilitator is trained to guide participants through a series of questions, inviting participation via chat, and raising hands using the Zoom feature.

Example: I produce several events a year for Feeding America, a nonprofit that partners with 200 affiliated food banks in the US. When it was time for the contract to be renewed, the organization gathered food bank CEOs into smaller, facilitated groups to discuss proposed changes. An assigned notetaker captured that feedback.

Save Breakout Room assignments for future use
For a recurring meeting, you can save the breakout room assignments so the same participants are together the next time the group meets. After setting up rooms, but before opening them, click on the **three dots (. . .)** on the bottom of the window and select **Save Breakout Rooms**. You may only save a maximum of 10 configurations.[2]

WHAT STYLE OF BREAKOUT ROOM WORKS BEST?

There are three options to choose from when setting up breakout rooms:

- Assign automatically (randomly)
- Assign manually (make specific assignments)
- Let participants choose their rooms

As you might have guessed, the answer to which style to choose depends on what outcome you're trying to achieve. For each style, I'll describe the style and provide an example.

Co-host can move between rooms
No matter which style you select, the host and co-hosts can always move between all the breakout rooms. One of my clients ran a weekly employee engagement event on Zoom that included two breakout room segments. The CEO moved between rooms to say a quick hello throughout the 15-minute session while the rest of the participants stayed in their automatically assigned (randomly assigned) rooms.
To switch rooms, the host/co-host clicks on the **Breakout Rooms** button at the bottom of their Zoom window and clicks the **Join** button next to the room to which they want to move.

Assign Automatically

This is the default style and will assign participants randomly to rooms.

How to Assign Automatically

- After joining a Zoom meeting as the host or co-host, click on the **Breakout Rooms** button on the bottom of the Zoom window.

- As you adjust the number of rooms to open, Zoom calculates at the bottom of the window how many participants per room, based on the number of participants in the main room at that time.

- Click on the **Create** button.

- Click on the gear icon on the bottom left of the next screen to adjust breakout room options.

- If you pre-set the breakout rooms several minutes before they will open, hit the **Recreate** button right before opening them. Anyone who joined since the rooms were set up will be assigned.

- Optional: Click **Add Room** button three times to have three empty rooms available if several latecomers join right after the breakout rooms open.

- Click the **Open All Rooms** button.

> *The number of participants per room should depend on the purpose of the breakout room activity, considering the max number of rooms is currently 50 and will soon be 100.*

If the max number of rooms available is 50:

If you have 250 or fewer participants, you can easily set up rooms with four to five participants.

If you have between 250-400 participants, you can still use breakout rooms but may need to assign seven or eight people for 15 minutes to give everyone adequate time to respond to the prompt.

If you have more than 400 participants, breakout rooms would strongly benefit from an assigned facilitator, because you will need to put more than eight people into breakout rooms for more than 15 minutes.

Breakout room limit increasing from 50 to 100

As I write this book, Zoom announced 100 breakout rooms will become the default. They then delayed this update. If you don't have access to this feature yet, it can be requested for your account by the administrator (even before it becomes the default maximum).

1. Log into www.Zoom.us.

2. Click on the ChatBot in the bottom right corner of any Zoom page and ask your question.

    a. You can access live chat if you have a Business or Enterprise account (or pay more than $50 a month for a Pro account).

    b. Otherwise, if you ask a question that the ChatBot can't resolve, it will share the link to submit a ticket in a reply message.

If the max number of rooms available is 100:

If you have 500 or fewer participants, you can easily set up rooms with four to five participants.

If you have between 500-800 participants, you can still use breakout rooms, but may need to assign seven or eight people for 15 minutes to give everyone adequate time to respond to the prompt.

If you have more than 800 participants, breakout rooms would strongly benefit from an assigned facilitator, because you will need to put more than eight people into breakout rooms for more than 15 minutes.

There's no reason to do math when setting up breakout rooms. Decide ahead of time how many participants per room, then adjust the number of rooms until you see the number you had in mind at the bottom of the pop-up window. That's it. No more needing to think out loud, "Let's see . . . we have 22 people, so we'll need four rooms. No, five rooms . . . Hmm, wait, that would be . . ."

Instead, decide whether you will go up by one or down by one if the rooms don't split evenly. If you plan for four per room, if the number of participants is uneven, would you prefer three to four per room or four to five per room?).

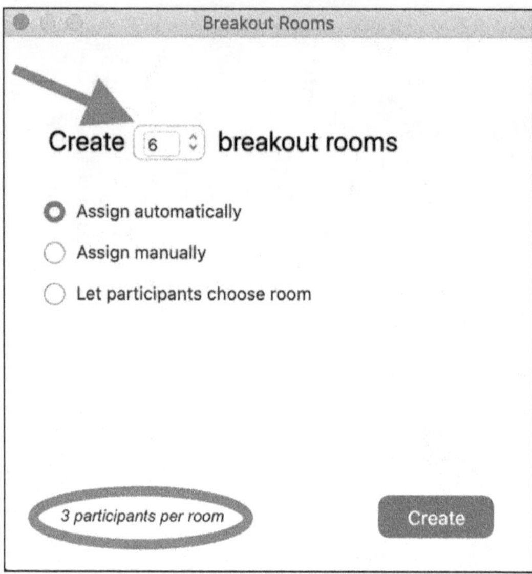

FIGURE 6.4. The number of participants per room will change as you increase or decrease the number of rooms and will be based on the total number of participants in the main room at that moment. If 18 participants are in the main room and six breakout rooms are created, there will be three participants per room. If you'd prefer six participants per room, decrease the number of rooms to three.

DEALING WITH UNASSIGNED PARTICIPANTS

In April 2020, I participated in a Zoom event that started with breakout rooms. This was a breath of fresh air, because at that time, most organizations were not including breakout rooms in their event design.

The meeting host wasn't experienced with Zoom, so she sought guidance ahead of time and wrote out the steps. She set up the breakout rooms and opened them about five minutes after the meeting began. Of the 40+ people in the main room, 12 of us didn't get sent to a breakout room. I was in that group. Nervous that she had done something wrong, she immediately closed the breakout rooms. Unfortunately, they still had the default sixty-second countdown once the rooms closed, so there was a bit of a delay between when she closed the rooms and when participants appeared in the main room.

When participants returned to the main room, there were quite a few chuckles about how quickly those 15 minutes flew by and a request by the lead organizer to send everyone back to the breakout rooms. The host again opened the breakout rooms, and once again, 12 of us stayed behind in the main room. Before she went through this again, I unmuted and asked her to make me the host, as I knew how to fix this without closing the breakout rooms. She gratefully did that.

I realized the problem. She had set up the breakout rooms before everyone arrived. Twelve participants joined the meeting after that point and were unassigned. To fix this, I opened the breakout room list window and found 12 names at the top in the Unassigned section. One by one, I moved each participant into an existing breakout room. The only problem was that each room already had six participants, so it felt like I was squeezing in one more.

For this reason, I always recommend that you do two things before opening breakout rooms that have been automatically assigned:

1. Click the **Recreate** button. You'll find this button on the same pop-up window as the **Open All Rooms** button. Clicking the **Recreate** button will take you back to the screen where you selected how many rooms to open. Look at the Zoom calculated number of participants per room at the bottom of that screen and then adjust the number of rooms if necessary.

2. Just in case, click the **Add Room** button three times (this is on that same screen next to the **Open All Rooms** button). This way, you will have empty rooms if you need to assign several latecomers who arrive right after you open the breakout rooms.

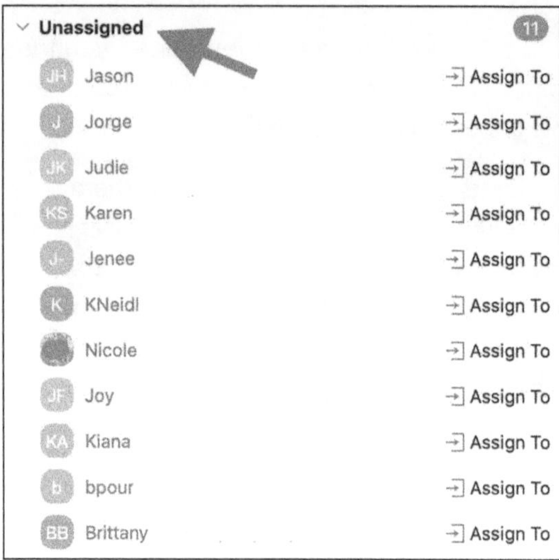

FIGURE 6.5. After opening breakout rooms, look at the top of the **Breakout Rooms** window and check to see if anyone is **Unassigned** who shouldn't be. Clicking **Assign To** places them in a breakout room.

Enable new breakout room setting

As of March 2023, I recommend enabling a new breakout room setting **Create, rename, and delete breakout rooms when rooms are open**. If you end up with several late-arriving participants right after you open the breakout rooms, you can easily open additional rooms and manually assign those participants.

If you don't see this in **Zoom.us Settings**, this feature needs to be requested for your account by the administrator.

1. Log into www.Zoom.us.

2. Click on the ChatBot in the bottom right corner of any Zoom page and ask your question.

   a. You can access live chat if you have a Business or Enterprise account (or pay more than $50 a month for a Pro account).

   b. Otherwise, if you ask a question that the ChatBot cannot resolve, it will share the link to submit a ticket in a reply message.

*Why did I wait to recommend this setting? I was waiting for the minimum Zoom version required by the **Zoom Software Quarterly Lifecycle Policy**[3] to be higher than the minimum required for this feature, because every participant needs to have the minimum version, or they won't be able to join the meeting if the setting is enabled.*[4]

Assign Manually

If more than a handful of participants need to be assigned to specific rooms, use this room style to place everyone exactly where they need to be.

How to Assign Manually

- After joining a Zoom meeting as the host or co-host, click on the **Breakout Rooms** button at the bottom of the Zoom window.

- Adjust the number of rooms to match the number you want to open.

- Select the second option: **Assign Manually**.

- Click on the **Create** button.

- The Breakout Rooms window will open, and all participants will be listed alphabetically in the **Unassigned** section at the top of the window.

- Optional: Next to each **Room**, select **Rename** and type in or copy/paste the topic (a maximum of 32 characters).

- Miscounted and need additional rooms? Click **Add Room** button.

- Click **Assign** next to each participant to place them in one of the rooms you previously opened.

- *Do not recreate rooms - all assignments and labels will disappear!*

- Click on the gear icon on the bottom left of the next screen to adjust breakout room **Options**.

- Click the **Open All Rooms** button.

In Chapter One, I shared a story about an event I produced with a complicated breakout room exercise that required 300 participants to be divided into 30 rooms with an assigned facilitator AND grouped by one of six self-selected topics.

This part of the event began with about 15 minutes of presentation, which included a request for each participant to update their Zoom name to include a three-letter code that indicated to which of the six topics they wanted to be assigned for the second breakout room.

The host can rename a participant
Open the **Participant** window, hover over the participant's name, and click on the **More** button to see the **Rename** option. This can also be done by clicking on the **three dots (. . .)** on the top right of a participant's video.

For the first breakout rooms segment, I needed to set up 30 rooms of ten participants with an assigned facilitator. I asked each facilitator to put an * in front of their name, so they were at the top of the

Unassigned list when I used the **Assigned Manually** style to set up the breakout rooms. After moving the 30 facilitators to their assigned rooms, I then manually assigned all the other participants to the 30 rooms, making sure there was a maximum of 10 per room. These were random assignments—meaning it did not matter which room each participant was in once the facilitators were properly assigned.

When they returned from this breakout room, there was time for a 10-minute debrief and then a 15-minute break. During this time, I set up the second, more complex, breakout room.

By this point, most participants had put a three-letter code before their name. Once again, I used the **Assign Manually** style, and I started by assigning the facilitators. I then used the three-letter code to manually assign participants to breakout rooms, which I renamed to help me keep track of which rooms were which topics. If a participant joined during this process, their name appeared in the **Unassigned** section of the list, and I contacted them via chat to ask to which topic they wanted to be assigned.

Need to fill in last-minute arrivals?
Did someone join the Zoom meeting after you've carefully constructed your breakout rooms? Don't want to hit recreate to sweep the new person into the mix? Simply hover over the blue number next to the breakout room to which you want to add the new arrival and click **Assign**. When the small pop-up window appears, unassigned participants will be listed with a checkbox. Check this box to assign a participant to this room. All the other assignments stayed the same.

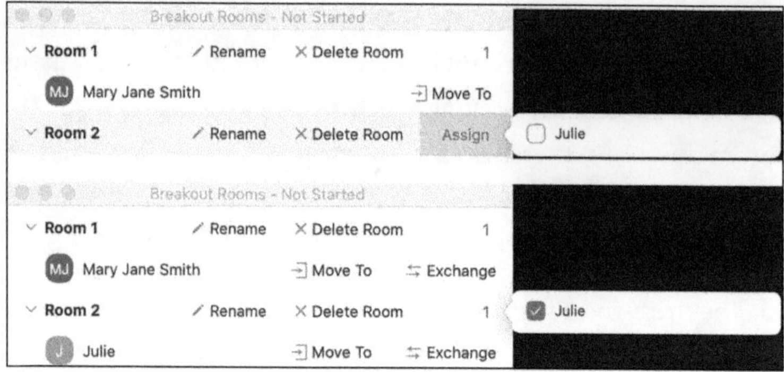

FIGURE 6.6. Hover over the number of participants in a room, click on **Assign,** and any unassigned participants will be listed with a checkbox. Check the box, and they will be assigned to that room.

*What if you want to keep someone in the main room when breakout rooms open and they're not a co-host? Click **Assign** next to the room they are currently and uncheck the box next to their name.*

Locate participant in a breakout room

If you need to double-check that a participant or facilitator is in the correct room after breakout rooms are open, you no longer need to scan through each room's list of participants. Click the **Participants** tab at the top of the **Breakout Rooms** window. All participants (including co-hosts) are listed alphabetically with their room number in the second column. From here, you can move a participant to a different room.

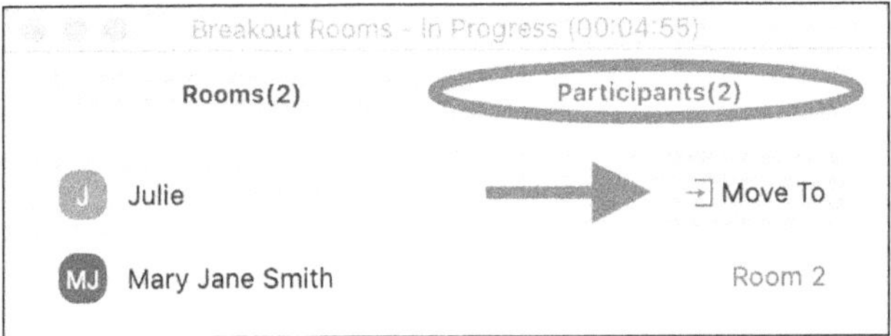

FIGURE 6.7. After breakout rooms are opened, Zoom has a feature that alphabetizes all participants (and co-hosts) by first name so you can easily find them and manually move them to a different room. This is helpful if you've assigned each facilitator to a specific room.

Moving Participants Between Rooms

As I was reviewing the breakout rooms I'd set up for this complex breakout room exercise, I noticed that I had accidentally assigned a few participants to the wrong rooms. If this happens to you, don't panic! It's simple to move a participant to a different room:

1. Look at each breakout room's list to find the participant who needs to be moved.

2. Click **Move** next to that participant. On the small pop-up window, select the new room.

That's it! They'll be moved to the other room, and everyone else stays where they were assigned.

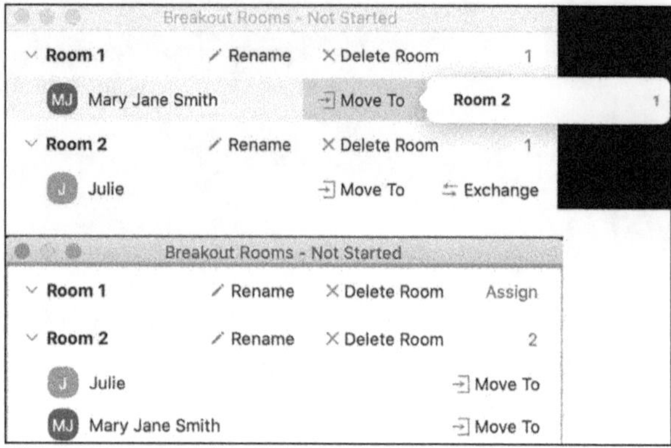

FIGURE 6.8. In this example, Mary Jane Smith moves from Room 1 to Room 2 by clicking on **Move To** and selecting Room 2.

One note of caution: Moving a participant to a new room AFTER the rooms have been opened can be quite disconcerting for them. They're in a conversation, then suddenly, they're yanked away and thrust into a brand new room. Avoid this by making these adjustments BEFORE opening the rooms. If you realize you need to make an adjustment more than 10 seconds after the rooms have opened, I recommend joining the room to interrupt the conversation and explain what you're about to do. It's a bit disruptive, but less jarring than making the switch without this heads-up.

PRE- ASSIGN BREAKOUT ROOMS

This is a feature that allows you to upload a CSV file with breakout room assignments before the Zoom meeting begins. Enable this breakout room feature at **Zoom.us Settings**, and an option to pre-assign breakout rooms will appear when scheduling a meeting. For this to work, you'll need a list of participants and the email address they use to access Zoom.

In theory, this would save a lot of time during the meeting and replace the effort of **Assigning Manually**. In my experience, there are some downsides to this feature that have led me to dissuade clients from using it.

- If you open up breakout rooms earlier in the event that don't use the pre-assigned list, this will wipe out your pre-assignment.

- Participants must be logged in using the same email address you used to pre-assign them, or they won't be assigned to any breakout room.

The number of participants in a Zoom meeting often drops right before the breakout rooms are opened. This might lead to very uneven numbers of participants if you keep the pre-assignments.

You could plan to start with pre-assignments and then manually make adjustments to fix the second and third problems, but as I described earlier in this chapter, **Assigning Manually** sorts participants by alphabet and makes this process fairly smooth. I prefer this option because it still allows me to open breakout rooms earlier in the event that don't use the pre-assigned list. You may want to be able to have randomly assigned breakout rooms for an icebreaker, even if you're planning to divide participant into specific teams later in the event for a discussion or deep dive.

Let Participants Choose Room

Use this style if the goal is to give participants the ability to select which conversations they want to join.

How to set up a "choose your own adventure" activity

After joining a Zoom meeting as the host or co-host, click on the **Breakout Rooms** button on the bottom of the Zoom window.

- Adjust the number of rooms to match the number of topics.

- Select the third option: **Let participants choose room.**

- Click on the **Create** button.

- Next to each **Room**, select **Rename** and type in or copy/paste the topic (a maximum of 32 characters).

- *Do not recreate rooms - all labels will disappear!*

- Click on the gear icon on the bottom left of the **Breakout Rooms** window to adjust breakout room **Options**.

- Click the **Open All Rooms** button.

- Give instructions to participants, so they understand how to join a room and move between rooms (see the next sidebar).

- Enable the **Waiting Room** as a security precaution. Any participant who joins once these breakout rooms are open can immediately join a room and be disruptive. It's also nice to welcome latecomers and explain what's happening. This is why I recommend that you manually admit each participant in from the **Waiting Room** during this exercise. Click on the **Security** badge and click on **Enable Waiting Room** to add a checkmark.

INSTRUCTIONS FOR PARTICIPANTS CHOOSE ROOMS

If you're giving participants a long list of topic choices, I recommend sharing that list in chat or on a shared slide. In my experience, even when given this information in advance, participants need time to decide before joining a breakout room. I've learned to add a two minute buffer for this exercise (e.g., 17 minutes instead of 15 minutes) to account for this delay.

Once you open the breakout rooms, explain to participants that they should look for the **Breakout Rooms** button on the bottom right of their Zoom window. Once they click that, they'll see a list of rooms with topics. To join any of these rooms, they click on the **Join** button next to that room. They'll be able to see who is in each room and can click on the **Breakout Rooms** button again once in the room to move to a different room.

If a participant is joining via a mobile device (cell phone or iPad), they'll need to tap their Zoom window and the **Breakout Rooms** button will appear on the top left of their screen. Mobile users won't be able to see who's in each room or how many people are there. They'll be able to move from room to room by clicking again on the **Breakout Rooms** button and selecting a new room.

The meeting host and co-host may manually move any participant from the main room into a breakout room or from one room to another.

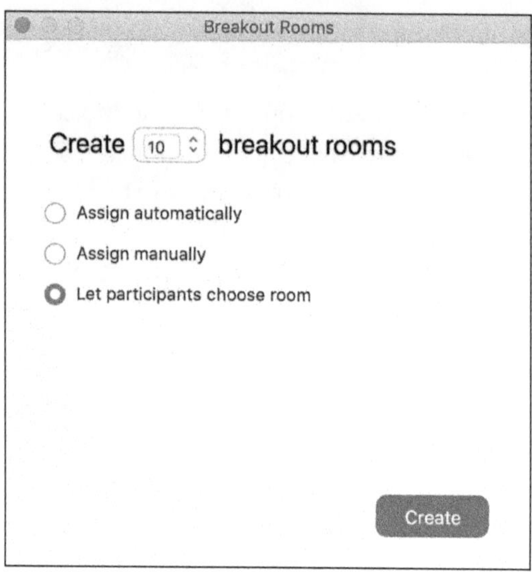

FIGURE 6.9. Remember to select **Let participants choose room** to set up this type of breakout room.

Avoid this mistake when letting participants choose
Do not select the first option: **Assign automatically** and then check **Allow participants** to choose room under the breakout room **Options** on the next screen (the gear on the bottom left corner). What will happen if you do? Participants will be automatically assigned to a random breakout room topic and won't realize that they have the ability to move between breakout rooms to choose a different topic.

There are pros and cons to using this method.

Pros: Serendipity is possible in virtual! Strategically designing breakout rooms with this style allows participants to literally find their people and have the kinds of conversations they want to have. Participants are able to join rooms, knowing there will be people to meet who have shared interests, identities, or challenges.

If one conversation isn't working for them, they can easily switch to another room.

Cons: You can't limit the number of people who join each room, so it's possible that you can end up with dozens of people in one of the rooms and only three in another. This is one of the reasons I couldn't use this style to solve the problem of having participants choose a room based on one of six topics. With 300 participants, I needed to control where participants were assigned to keep room capacity to 10 participants.

Zoom recently released a feature that creates breakout rooms based on poll results. That would be another way to have participants select a topic for their breakout room discussion.[5]

Poll results can create breakout room assignments
Select this option as you set up a poll or view poll results.[6] Unlike the **Let participants choose room style**, you can decide how many participants you want in each breakout room. You can also manually move participants around after you create the rooms.

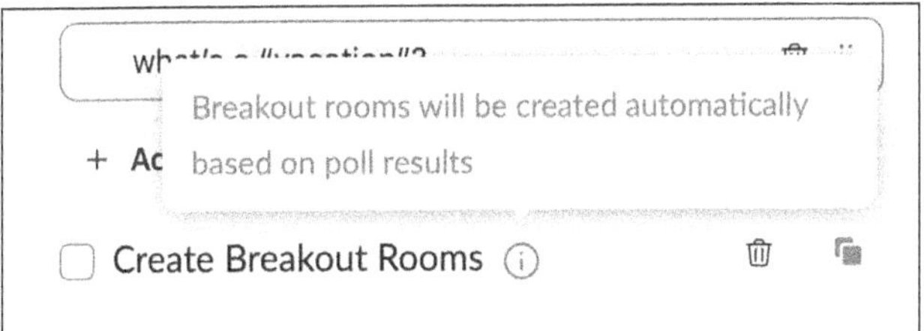

FIGURE 6.10. Check (✓) **Create Breakout Rooms** when you add the poll question.

Here's an example. On March 13, 2020, I hosted my first virtual happy hour. I hosted #NoMoreBadZoom Virtual Happy Hour weekly from March 2020 to April 2022, when it became a monthly event held on the first Friday of the month. Early on, it was a great opportunity to test out Zoom features.

This is a free networking event for entrepreneurs with the objective of building relationships and showing participants how to design and facilitate engaging online events. To help us achieve the first objective, the event includes several breakout room segments. The last is a "choose your own adventure" breakout room where participants can move between ten topics.

The topics include marketing challenges, writing/launching a book, and launching an online course. I have one room dedicated to our guest expert's presentation for those who'd like to dig deeper into that topic or ask additional questions. This breakout room style allows for the discovery of common and uncommon connections. Generally, having breakout rooms is what has allowed event participants to become community members. Those community connections over the last three years have led to friendships and business partnerships across time zones.

You're welcome to join us! We meet on the first Friday of every month at 5 p.m. ET. It's a great way to experience a fun and engaging virtual event. Plus, you get to ask me questions during the 30 minute Q&A at the end of each event. Register (it's free) at www.NoMoreBadZoom.com.

CREATING INTENTIONAL ENGAGEMENT IN BREAKOUT ROOMS

I keep saying breakout rooms have the power to transform a virtual event into an almost magical space filled with serendipity, but we have all experienced that dreaded moment at the start of breakout rooms when everyone is on mute and no one knows who should take the lead.

That moment always feels a bit awkward, especially if the reason we're all in the breakout rooms to begin with wasn't made clear, and none of us knows what we should be discussing or how long we'll be left on our own. As I've said, someone will eventually unmute and some other participants may join in, but this setup is quite lacking and doesn't feel welcoming to all participants.

> *Doing only the minimum effort in design and facilitation results in only some participants feeling comfortable sharing. I call this checkbox engagement. It's not enough, and it leaves participants craving more.*

Here are steps to take to shift this exercise from checkbox engagement to intentional engagement:

Always start with the end in mind.

You're probably not surprised to hear that before opening the breakout rooms, you need to have a clear purpose for them. Once you've decided how these breakout room conversations will help participants move toward the desired outcome, then you'll have a much better chance of determining what question they should answer or which prompt they should discuss.

You don't have to overthink this, though. If the breakout room is in the middle of a training session, it can be time for participants to share their biggest takeaway thus far, engage in role playing, discuss the content, or work through content in small groups.

Wondering if participants are engaged in breakout rooms? It's not possible to be a fly on the wall while all the breakout room conversations are taking place. However, it's possible to view the list of open breakout rooms to see if participants have their cameras on, are sharing their screen, or if they're using reactions (emojis) or nonverbal feedback. Enable this feature at **Zoom.us Settings: Allow host to view activity statuses of participants in breakout rooms**. Participants are notified when breakout rooms open that their activity status is being shared with the host.

FIGURE 6.11. With this setting enabled, the host can see that Mary Jane turned on her camera in the breakout room.

What's THE Breakout Room Question?

If there's no assigned facilitator, give participants *a single question* for each breakout room segment. Please do *not* give them a list of questions from which to choose. That shifts the responsibility of a well-designed experience from you to the participants. It often includes confusing instructions that don't lead to the kinds of conversations you're hoping they will have.

Engage more deeply

If you're looking for questions to use for icebreakers or to foster connection, I recommend the www.AskDeepQuestions.com card deck created by Jan Keck. They range from light-hearted curious questions, to slightly adventurous brave questions, to deeply vulnerable questions.[7]

Another resource I recommend is Climer Cards created by Dr. Amy Climer. These are available for virtual or in-person events, and they're a great tool to help people move to a deeper level of conversation. The deck of cards includes a wide array of images (hand-painted by Amy) that participants select in response to a question. They then share why they selected that card. The question can be light: "Select a card that represents what you were hoping to get out of today's session?" or it can go much deeper, depending on your content.[8]

FIGURE 6.12. Climer Cards, like the ones pictured, are used to create a deeper conversation. Free 30-day trial and 10% discount available at <u>www. ClimerCards.com</u> (use promocode Robbie10 at checkout).

If you have more than one question that would work well in a breakout room format, you can always give participants 10 minutes to discuss the first question, bring them back to the main room to debrief (I'll share my debrief strategies below), then send them back to breakout rooms for the second question, and so on.

You can keep participants assigned to the same room for each segment or mix them up. Your decision to keep or mix should be based on the purpose of the breakout room segments. Are participants meant to dig deeper and share more personal anecdotes each time they reconvene? If so, keep them in the same room assignments. Is networking a primary or secondary reason to have breakout rooms? Then switch up the assignments for each segment.

Roleplaying with an audience

Giving participants an opportunity to roleplay is a powerful way to have them embody your content and prepare them for taking action after the session ends. If you have fewer than 150 participants and a maximum of 50 rooms (or fewer than 300 participants with a maximum 100 rooms), you can set up breakout rooms with three participants, where one is observing while the other two are roleplaying. During the debrief, ask each participant in the roleplay about their experience. Ask the participant who was observing what they noticed. If there's time available, place them back into breakout rooms and switch who is the observer.

UNINTENDED CONSEQUENCES

In 2020, I attended dozens of virtual networking events to experience a variety of event designs and see how I could improve my own participants' experience at my weekly #NoMoreBadZoom Virtual Happy Hour.[9] One of these events underscored the importance of my "one question" strategy when they assigned seven participants to a breakout room for 15 minutes and gave us THREE questions to answer.

The first question was "Share a challenge that you're facing," which meant the first person to unmute got 12 minutes of support from the other six members—until I realized only three minutes were left, at which point we quickly did 30-second intros from the rest of us.

If the purpose of that breakout room had been to provide feedback for one of the members (such as a mastermind with one participant in the "hot seat"), then this setup might have worked, but it was a networking event, so participants believed these breakout rooms were meant to give them an opportunity to get to know each other and that didn't happen.

Share a Challenge

If it's important that challenges get discussed in breakout rooms without assigned facilitators, frame the question this way: "Share a challenge you faced and how you overcame it."

That way, participants realize they're not the only one to have had this challenge, and they learn coping strategies. A bonus of this framing is that participants get to witness and celebrate other participants' resilience while receiving acknowledgment for their own.

Use Technology to Communicate

"OK. Now I'm going to send you into breakout rooms for about 10 minutes."

Participants are then sent into breakout rooms with no countdown clock and seemingly randomly timed broadcast messages stating how much time is left and that the rooms are now closing.

This leaves participants wondering how much time they'll actually get and how much time is remaining as each person takes their turn.

Instead, use Zoom's breakout room options to clearly communicate this information to participants while they're in the room. On the screen with the **Open All Rooms** button, click on the gear on the bottom left corner to adjust options:

- **Auto close breakout rooms after ___ minutes**

- **Set countdown timer: ___ seconds**

For example, **Auto close breakout rooms after 10 minutes** and **Set countdown timer: 15 seconds.**

(Refer to the **How to Set Up Breakout Room** section of this book if you have questions about the other breakout room options.)

Once the breakout rooms are opened, there are three ways to communicate with participants in those rooms: through broadcast message, broadcast voice, or by sharing your screen.

Broadcast Message

This is the least intrusive way to send a message to all breakout rooms. Click on the **Broadcast** button on the **Breakout Rooms** window. Select **Broadcast Message**, type in the message, and click the arrow to submit. Your message will appear in a small font at the top of the screen in each breakout room for about 10 seconds.[10]

> *Keep messages short, as long messages are difficult to read quickly. The in-person comparison is the facilitator walking past groups holding up a sign that says, "Two minutes left!"*

Broadcast Voice

This feature allows you to use your microphone to send an audio message to all breakout rooms. Click on **Broadcast** button on the **Breakout Rooms** window, select **Broadcast Voice**. Click the blue voice icon to begin transmitting your microphone and click the red stop icon to stop. Use this sparingly, since this feature interrupts the conversation. The in-person comparison is the facilitator walking up to each group, leaning in and saying, "Two minutes left!"

Share Screen

You can share slides, whiteboard, or audio and video from the main room to the breakout rooms. This feature could be very useful if your plan is to have participants watch something while in the breakout rooms and then immediately discuss what they viewed. Paired with an assigned facilitator, screen sharing from the main room would ensure that every breakout room is moving through slides at the same pace and that they each have the same amount of time for discussion before the rooms are closed. It's possible to share video from a file on your computer or share computer sound when browsing a website or YouTube.[11] You can share a slide or **Whiteboard** with participants in the breakout rooms to send a written message, although participants cannot annotate.

First, send participants into breakout rooms. Then click **Share Screen** and at the bottom of the pop-up window ✓ the box for **Share to breakout rooms** and ✓ the box for **Share sound**.

*Explain to participants that while you are sharing your screen into the breakout rooms, they can use **Side-by-side Mode** to make participant videos fill up most of the screen and make the slide or video you are sharing smaller. To confirm they have this setting enabled, share the slide while in the main room and tell them that if the slide is on the left side of their screen and you are on the right, they are all set. If not, guide them to click the **View Options** drop-down at the top middle of the screen next to the green bar that says, "You are viewing so-and-so's screen" and select **Side-by-side Mode** from the list. This view becomes the default whenever someone shares their screen. Participants can make the slide bigger or smaller by dragging the dividing line left or right.[12]*

Can I send a chat message to participants in breakout rooms
Nope. If you've already opened the breakout rooms it's too late to post a message into the main room chat that's meant to be read by all participants. Chat messages are only visible to participants who're in the room when the message was posted. If they join the room later, they won't see the message that was posted in their absence.

The same is true for messages written in chat while in the breakout rooms. Only other participants in the main room at that time will be able to view that message.

Get Participants Brains Engaged

Even when you have a thoughtfully selected question, that doesn't mean participants will discuss that question once in the breakout rooms. For that to happen, we need to get them thinking about their answer *before* the rooms even open. Doing so will greatly improve the participant experience in those rooms.

Use this two-step process to get their brains engaged, so they're primed to share stories related to the question you ask.

- **Say the question or prompt.** The presenter or facilitator reads aloud the question or prompt, even if it's visible on a slide.

- **Answer the question or prompt.** That same person or a pre-selected participant shares their answer to the question or prompt.

Example: "In the breakout rooms, I'd like you to take two minutes to share your biggest professional win this week. To kick us off, I'll share mine…"

Who Goes First?

To avoid that awkward moment at the start of a breakout room, suggest a speaking order. Tread cautiously here, or you'll choose something that takes time away from the discussion. Avoid subjective or difficult-to-discern identifiers such as hair length, darkness/lightness of clothing, or birthday. Participants will end up discussing how one of the participants is bald, whether blue or green is darker, or getting sidetracked by horoscopes.

Keep things simple by asking participants to go in alpha order by first name, alpha order by last name, or reverse alpha by first or last name. Switch this up for each breakout room segment, so participants with names closer to the start of the alphabet aren't always going first.

Would your breakout room exercise benefit if participants shared in a particular order? Perhaps you'd like more experienced participants to share first? If that's the case, give the instruction that all participants should write how many years of experience they have in chat as soon as they join the breakout room. That will make it easy to determine the order quickly and allow participants to use more time to discuss the topic you selected.

Last names not showing?

"Please answer this prompt in alpha order by last name. If your last name is not visible, then you're going first." This often leads to a quick effort by participants to update their Zoom name to include their first and last name!

As You Open the Room

Let's do a quick review checklist:

- Read the question or prompt aloud.

- Have someone share their answer as an example/model for how it should be done.

- Set the number of minutes in **Options**.

- Set the countdown timer to 15 seconds.

Right before opening breakout rooms:

- Tell participants how many minutes total and per person.

- Tell participants the speaking order.

- Copy and paste question/prompt into **Chat**.

- **Recreate** rooms.*

- **Open All Rooms.**

   *Only recreate rooms if you've selected **Assigned Automatically.** *DO NOT RECREATE* rooms if you've selected **Assigned Manually** or **Let participants choose room**. If you do, you'll have to set up the rooms again.

Here's an example: *"Next, you'll be heading into a 10-minute breakout room to discuss this question. There will be four or five people per room, so that will leave about two minutes per person. A countdown clock will be available on the top right once you're in the breakout room. Let's go in reverse alphabetical order by first name. If you'd like to read the question again, click on chat when you're in the breakout rooms, and you'll see it's the last thing I posted. When time runs out, you'll have 15 seconds to wrap up your conversation before being automatically brought back to the main room for a full group debrief."*

BREAKOUT ROOM DEBRIEF

Most breakout room exercises will feel incomplete if you don't include time for a debrief. The debrief is an opportunity to hear from participants. The default debrief used by many speakers and facilitators is to invite participants to raise their hand and be called upon. I'm going to share several other options that will help diversify which voices are heard.

Nominations in Chat

When participants return from the breakout room, invite them to nominate someone in their group to share by writing that participant's name in chat. For example, if participants were sharing wins in the breakout room, you could say, "Did you hear a particularly compelling win that you think should be shared with all of us so we can celebrate with them? Nominate that person by writing their name in Chat and we'll invite them to unmute and briefly share their win."

What I love about this debrief option is that it isn't based on popularity or who is most outgoing. Participants are nominated if another participant found their answer or story useful, interesting, exciting, or in some other way compelling. The best responses rise up and anyone can be selected—even if this is their first time attending this event and no one knew them previously.

Type Takeaway in Chat

When participants return from the breakout room, invite them to share their thoughts in chat. If you're tight on time, this debrief can be done in just two minutes, Take five or even 10 minutes if you opt to call on some participants to share more about what they'd written in chat. Encourage participants to **Save Chat** if the comments would be helpful to review later.

Here's an example.

*"Welcome back everyone. Take a moment to write in chat your biggest takeaway from your discussion. What did you learn? Any ah-has? I see some responses coming in now. Let me read a few aloud. Don't forget to **Save Chat** so you'll be able to read all of these answers after the session. Click on the **three dots(. . .)** on the bottom of the Chat window and select **Save Chat**. Remember to do that again at the end of the event if you want to save everything shared in chat. This will be saved to your computer in the Documents folder in a Zoom folder. Ok, I'm scrolling back up to read aloud some of your responses. . ."*

Waterfall Debrief

This option is very similar to the previous one with one big difference—participants do not hit enter until you tell them to do so. The benefit of this is participants can carefully formulate their answer and type it into chat without their brain needing to read responses coming in at the same time. It's as close to an analog moment as you can get on a digital platform. Then, when you tell them to hit enter, all the answers come flooding in. You can then give participants a minute to scroll through the answers themselves, while you look for the ones you want to highlight by reading aloud or inviting that participant to unmute to share more of their answer.

For example, you have a breakout room with the question, *If you had free time, what would you like to learn?* Participants return to the room and write their answer into chat but wait to hit enter until you tell them to do so. After they hit enter, ask participants to scroll through chat, looking for answers that resonate with them—either because they have the same interest, or because they can share a resource to help another participant take action. I've had participants decide to meet up to practice language skills, or share YouTube channels with helpful musical instrument lessons. It's a great way to help participants find common interests with people who were not even in their breakout room.

Who Took Notes?

There are participants who naturally fall into the role of notetaker, because that's how they take in information. This often means they're not getting as much airtime as those participants who are more outgoing and less focused on notetaking. This debrief option invites those self-assigned note-takers to raise their hands to be called upon to share their top one or two takeaways or a brief update from their room.

What I love about this debrief option is how it gives the microphone to participants who may not have been inclined to raise their hand without notetaking being the context. It also brings some of the best ideas to the full group and honors the effort some participants make to take notes.

Me, Me, Me!

When participants return to the main room, invite them to queue up to share their takeaways by using the **Raise Hand** option under **Reactions**. This means participants are self-nominating to get airtime. This could be the perfect option to debrief your breakout room exercise—just don't let it be the default option. Always consider how the debrief will help move participants toward the desired outcome of thinking, feeling, or doing something differently.

Who's on-deck?

Queue up a few participants by asking them to use the **Raise Hands** function on Zoom, found under the **Reactions** button. That way, you can call on participants in an orderly fashion and let the next person know they're on-deck.

For example, "First, we're going to hear from Susan. Then we'll hear from Mary. Susan, go ahead and unmute to share your answer to this question." This on-deck method gives Mary a heads-up that she will be next, so she's ready to unmute when it's her turn. After Susan is done speaking, "Thanks, Susan. Next, we're going to hear from Mary and then Anne. Mary, go ahead and unmute to share your answer."

No one is caught off guard when it's their turn, and you can hear from more people because there are fewer delays caused by participants being slow to unmute themselves.

Asking participants to call on the next person to speak after their turn is over adds confusion and angst to what could be a simple process. The participant no one knows or who has a difficult-to-pronounce name gets picked last. Time is wasted trying to figure out who has already gone. Basically, you are handing over the facilitation process to participants and not taking responsibility for the group's experience.

Instead, open the Participants window, click the Mute All button, and participants will be listed alphabetically.[13] Tell participants you will be going either alphabetically or reverse alphabetically so they have a sense of when their turn will be. Verbally say who is on-deck or use the Ask to Unmute button to let participants know they are next.

BREAKOUT ROOM TIMING

Is there time for a breakout room exercise if you only have 60 minutes scheduled for your session? Possibly, but be careful not to miscalculate how much time a breakout room segment will take.

For example, a 10-minute breakout room exercise could take 17 minutes on your agenda. How? A 10-minute breakout + two minutes to share the question, example answer, and instructions + five minutes to debrief = 17 minutes.

Depending on which debrief option you choose, it could take as little as two minutes or closer to 20 minutes. If you were debriefing a role-play, expect that to take two to three times as long as the role-play exercise.

For that reason, it is much easier to fit a breakout room segment into a 75 or 90-minute session.

Nearly 20% of this book is dedicated to leveraging breakout rooms because I believe that with thoughtful planning, this feature has the potential to create transformative, welcoming, and intentionally engaging online experiences.

I would love to hear how you've used the strategies in this chapter to design your virtual session and how it went for your participants. If you have questions and would like to schedule a Speaker Strategy Session, reach out by sending a message to action@BreakOutofBoredom.com.

CHAPTER SEVEN

Speaker Checklists

Producing or hosting an event with multiple speakers? There are two opportunities to set speakers up for success: during a tech rehearsal several days or even a week before the event, and during the green room right before the event begins.

Ideally, during the green room, you're just confirming that everything you discussed during the rehearsal is in place. For that reason, it's important that speakers attend the tech rehearsal in the same location and using the same A/V equipment that they'll be using during your event. This will help avoid last-minute tech concerns.

> *If a speaker joins the tech rehearsal from their cell phone while in their car, there's no way to confirm their setup for the event. In these cases, I recommend the speaker send in a 30-second video clip, so their A/V setup can be reviewed before the event.*

What to discuss with speakers during these two meetings is similar but different enough that I've created distinct checklists to be sure all points are covered. Many points on these lists have been discussed in greater detail in other parts of this book. Check the *Table of Contents* if you need more information.

Download checklists
These checklists, and other resources to help you manage your event, are available as a PDF at www.robbiesamuels.com/breakout.

TECH REHEARSAL CHECKLIST

"Just in case" Text Thread

✓ Collect cell numbers from speakers in chat for the "just in case" text thread on the day of the event.

A/V check

✓ *"Say your full name and share what you had for breakfast"* is my go-to prompt for soundcheck.

✓ How does their audio sound? Too low compared to everyone else? Zoom **Audio Settings** has automatic and manual ways of adjusting audio levels. Tweak those settings to adjust the volume.

✓ If it appears they're using an external microphone, does the audio sound like it's coming from an external microphone? If not, the audio input needs to be adjusted.

Eye Contact

✓ Explain the importance of eye contact with the camera to engage participants.

✓ Demonstrate what it looks like to participants when the speaker looks at participant videos instead of the camera.

✓ Suggest various ways to draw their eye back to the camera (e.g., tape, photo, arrows, googly eyes).

✓ Talk about where their notes will be in relation to the camera, so they don't have to look at a second screen or the bottom of their screen to read their notes.

✓ Tell speakers they're visible—even when they're sharing their slides.

✓ Let them know someone else will be moderating chat, so they don't have to look at chat while presenting.

Video Check

✓ If they're using a laptop, is it propped up on books or a box, so the camera is at eye level?

✓ Are they sitting up nice and tall in the center of the screen?

✓ Can you see their torso? If they're only visible from the neck up, move the camera about an arm's length away.

✓ Is the angle of the camera showing the ceiling? Adjust so only two fingers of space can be seen above the speaker's head.

Participant Window

✓ When they're presenting, the speaker can open the **Participant** window to see the order that participants raise their hands.

✓ If they hear background noise, the speaker can click on the **Mute All** button (rather than talking about hearing background noise). This will mute everyone except the person who clicked the button, so it should only be used by the active speaker, or they'll accidentally mute the speaker.

Slides

✓ Are there slides? Who will share slides?

✓ Generally, encourage speakers to manage their own slides, as they'll know when to advance to the next slide and your participants won't need to hear "next slide" every few minutes.

✓ A copy of the final slides should be submitted ahead of time (two days to a week in advance is common). If the speaker has trouble sharing slides during the event, tell them who [producer, host, chat moderator] will share on their behalf.

✓ Does the speaker sharing their screen only have one monitor? Walk them through how to share a full screen PowerPoint while viewing the Speaker Notes. Telling them in advance gives them time to practice. (These steps are available in the *Lecture* section of the *Content* chapter and as a PDF at www.robbiesamuels. com/breakout.)

Polls

✓ Will any speakers be using polls?

✓ If yes, poll questions and answers need to be submitted ahead of time (two days to a week in advance is common).

Breakout Rooms

✓ Will any speakers be using breakout rooms?

✓ Discuss the purpose of the breakout rooms to help the speaker determine how many minutes and how many participants per room.

✓ Narrow the prompt to one question.

✓ Decide the speaking order.

✓ Add all this information to the run of show (ROS) document.

Links for Chat

✓ Are there any links or contact information that a speaker would like shared in chat during or at the end of their presentation?

✓ If yes, please share that information now in chat (we will ask this question again during the green room final tech check).

✓ Find out when during the program this information should be shared in chat, so it can be placed in the proper section of the ROS.

Discuss the Q&A Plan

✓ The goal is to keep the speaker's eyes on the camera most of the time, not reading chat.

✓ Who will track questions posted in chat?

✓ Will these questions be copied (with the participant's name) to a shared document (such as a Google doc)?

✓ Who will moderate the Q&A? In other words, who will pose questions to the speaker? Or will the speaker read the questions from the shared doc?

✓ Will speakers be taking questions live rather than via chat? If so, explain the importance of using Zoom's **Raise Hand** feature (under the **Reactions** button) and not saying, "Go ahead and unmute if you have any questions."

✓ Ask speakers to plan when they will check in with the chat moderator during their presentation to see if any pressing questions should be addressed before moving on to the next topic. Most questions will be held to the end.

✓ Tell speakers that the chat moderator is empowered to interject if a time-sensitive question is asked in chat.

GREEN ROOM CHECKLIST

"Just in case" text thread

✓ Confirm that each participant received and responded to the "just in case" text thread with their name. Having their name in the thread will make it easier to identify who might be contacting you with an issue if they don't include their name in their text.

A/V check

✓ Final sound check: *"Say your full name and share what you had for breakfast."*

✓ How does their audio sound? Too low compared to everyone else? Zoom **Audio Settings** has automatic and manual ways of adjusting audio levels. Tweak those settings to adjust the volume.

✓ If it appears they're using an external microphone, does the audio sound like it's coming from an external microphone? If not, the audio input needs to be adjusted.

Eye Contact

✓ Remind them about the importance of eye contact with the camera to engage participants.

✓ Confirm that their notes are close to their camera.

Final Video Check

✓ If they're using a laptop, is it propped up on books or a box, so the camera is at eye level?

✓ Are they sitting up nice and tall in the center of the screen?

✓ Can you see their torso? If only from the neck up, move the camera about an arm's length away.

✓ Is the angle of the camera showing the ceiling? Adjust so only two fingers of space can be seen above the speaker's head.

Make All Speakers Co-Hosts

✓ This makes it easier to find them in the Participant list to spotlight them. There's also a setting that allows you to choose whether all co-hosts are assigned to breakout rooms or kept in the main room.

✓ Explain to speakers that co-hosts cannot participate in polls but can accidentally end the poll prematurely. Identify who will launch polls, end polls, and share results as the speaker requests these actions (it can be the speaker if they're comfortable doing this).

✓ Tell speakers that as a co-host, they will see participants in the waiting room, but please *do not admit them*! Your host/ Zoom producer will disable the waiting room and admit all participants when we're ready, about two minutes before the event start time.

✓ Tell speakers not to remove any participants, as they won't be able to rejoin. If someone is disruptive, your host/Zoom producer will remove them.

Test Screen Sharing

Does the slide deck have embedded audio or video with sound? Remind the speaker sharing their screen to ✓ **Computer Sound** before sharing their screen. Advance to the slide with sound to confirm this setting is correct. This setting will now be the default for screen shares during this meeting.

During the tech rehearsal, did you share how to present a full screen PowerPoint with one monitor while viewing speaker notes? If yes, remind them of the steps and confirm that the speaker is comfortable with this setup. If they prefer to share their screen another way, now is not the time to convince them otherwise.

Order of operation for sharing slides on Zoom
Speakers should be able to access Zoom's floating toolbar (with Stop Share, Pause Share, etc.) when sharing their full screen presentation. The floating toolbar will not be visible if they put their slides into presentation mode before sharing their screen. If they pre-set their slides in the green room, they can smoothly share slides during the program without showing slides in setup mode and have access to the floating toolbar.

- To pre-set slides in the green room:

- In the green room, click **Share Screen** and share the slide deck in setup mode.

- Then press, **Play from Start** (PowerPoint), **Play** (Keynote), **Slideshow** (Google Slides), **Present** (Canva) to put slides into presentation mode.

- On the floating toolbar, click **Stop Share**.

- Once again, click **Share Screen** and share slide deck in presentation mode. This will be one of the options, and it will look like a full screen presentation of their first slide.

- Done in this order, the Zoom floating toolbar will be available when the presentation is full screen.

✓ Have the speaker Share Screen to show their slides.

– Confirm they selected a specific program to share and not their desktop.

– The file name will be visible (and should be ok for public view) if sharing PowerPoint using **Browsed by an individual (window)** or if they **Exit Full Screen** when sharing Google Slides. When sharing Keynote **In Window,** the file name doesn't show.

– The Google Slides presentation should be in a browser window by itself, if exiting full screen to share. Otherwise, extraneous browser tabs will be visible.

– Caution speakers against using Zoom's **Share Portion of Screen,** as this often results in parts of the speaker's desktop being shared by accident.

Participant Window

✓ Ask the speaker to open the **Participant** window to see the order in which participants raise their hands.

✓ Also, if they hear background noise, the speaker can click on the **Mute All** button on the bottom of the **Participant** window (rather than talking about hearing background noise). This will mute everyone except the person who clicked the button, so the active speaker should be the *only* one to use it, or they'll accidentally mute the speaker.

Review Polls

✓ Co-hosts can look at poll details to confirm that everything looks accurate—without launching the poll.

Run of Show Links

✓ Ask speakers to share any additional links or contact information in chat now, so this can be added to the run of show.

Confirm the Q&A Plan

✓ The goal is to keep the speaker's eyes on the camera most of the time, not reading chat.

✓ Confirm who will track questions posted in chat.

✓ If questions will be copied (with the participant's name) to a shared document (such as a Google Doc), has that doc been shared yet?

✓ Confirm who will moderate Q&A. Who will pose questions to the speaker? Or, will the speaker read the questions from the shared doc?

✓ Will speakers be taking questions live rather than via chat? Remind speakers to use the **Raise Hand** feature (under the **Reactions** button) to queue up questions rather than saying, "Go ahead and unmute if you have any questions."

✓ Remind speakers to check in with the chat moderator periodically to see if any pressing questions should be addressed before moving on to the next topic. Most questions will be held to the end.

✓ Remind speakers that the chat moderator is empowered to interject if a time-sensitive question is asked in chat.

Managing Microphone and Camera

✓ Speakers should be prepared to unmute themselves when it's their turn to speak. You'll be reminded to do so by a pop-up button after you've been put in the spotlight. Try to remember to mute yourself when you're done to reduce background noise during the next presentation. If necessary, your microphone will be muted for you.

✓ Speakers are asked to keep their camera on the entire time. If a video is off, that speaker can't be put in the spotlight. It's also helpful to fellow speakers to stay engaged the entire time and encourages participants to keep their own cameras on during your presentation.

I know it may seem like all this is unnecessary, since speakers have a lot of experience presenting virtually, but I can't tell you how many times I've been thanked for providing this level of support. I often hear from speakers that they received more guidance from me for this one virtual presentation than all other times they've been invited to speak. And that they plan to use this experience to help them improve their virtual presentations going forward.

I'd love to hear the feedback you receive from speakers—email action@ BreakOutofBoredom.com.

CHAPTER EIGHT

Safety & Security

As the host of a virtual meeting, it's your job to ensure that participants have a good experience. Keeping them safe from purposeful or accidental intrusions is an important part of that job.

In March and April 2020, as everyone shifted to hosting virtual meetings, it was common to see someone post their Zoom link on social media. It's no surprise that many of those early meetings were 'Zoom bombed,' meaning someone joined the meeting with the express intent of disrupting it.

Sharing a Zoom link publicly in 2020 was the equivalent of writing your phone number on a junior high school bathroom wall in 1980. You shouldn't be surprised if you receive crank calls asking, "Is your refrigerator running?" Except in the case of Zoom, these intrusions were not so mild. Some included screen shares with adult content, or crude drawings on shared screens.

This is one of the reasons I recommend that you do not use your Zoom Personal Meeting ID (PMI) for group meetings. That way, if a Zoom bomber interrupts your group meeting, you can easily change one group's link without having to resend the Zoom link to everyone who has been using your PMI link to join your meetings.

Personally, I only use my PMI for one-on-one calls. I've learned the importance of having the waiting room turned on, so if my next appointment arrives early, they don't accidentally disrupt my current appointment. Having a waiting room on at the start of each meeting is one way to lessen interruptions. Here are other settings to consider.

Are passcodes a security measure?
By default, Zoom embeds the passcode into the Zoom link. Anyone with the link joins the Zoom meeting without being prompted for a passcode. Embedding the passcode into the link is more convenient for participants, but does not provide any security.

For added security, you can disable the **Zoom.us Setting**: **Embed passcode in-meeting link for one-click join**. Expect slight delays to the start of your meeting while participants double-check their calendar invite or email inbox for the passcode.

PROFILE SECURITY SETTINGS

In the next chapter, I share a list of settings to enable, depending on whether you have a free or paid Zoom account. Here, I'm highlighting the settings that make your Zoom meetings safer by making it harder for Zoom bombers to be disruptive. The first step is to have these settings in place. Then you need to know how (and when) to use them.[1]

To get started, enable the following **Zoom.us Settings**,[2] which are available to all Zoom accounts. I've listed them in the order that they appear so you can start from the top of the Settings page and scroll down.

Waiting Room

Enable **Waiting Rooms** to be turned on by default to avoid a participant joining when you're not ready, or before you start the meeting. In the *Online Facilitation* chapter, I explain how (and why) to disable the waiting room once you're in the Zoom meeting and ready for participants.[3]

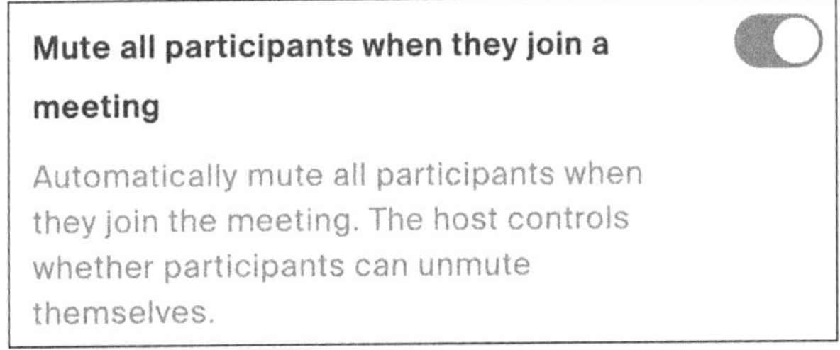

FIGURE 8.1. Enable the **Waiting Room** for all meetings.

Mute all participants when they join

Enable this setting so you won't have to deal with random background noise if participants join during your presentation.[4]

FIGURE 8.2. Enable this setting to prevent background noise as participants join the meeting.

> *Participants will still be able to unmute themselves. If you want to prevent participants from unmuting, see the **In Meeting Security Settings** section below.*

New Meeting Chat Experience

This allows you to delete chat messages if a participant writes something inappropriate.[5] As of the update on January 16, 2023, Zoom changed this to be enabled by default.

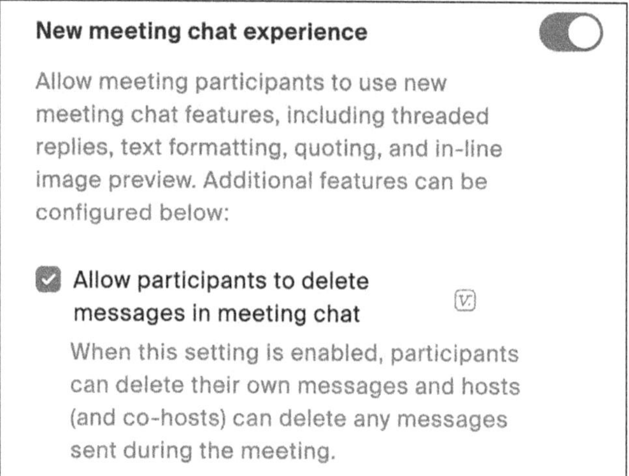

FIGURE 8.3. Confirm that **New meeting chat experience** is enabled so the host can delete chat messages.

Screen Sharing: Who Can Share? Select Host Only

By default, this setting is enabled for new Zoom accounts. Older accounts may need to enable this.[6]

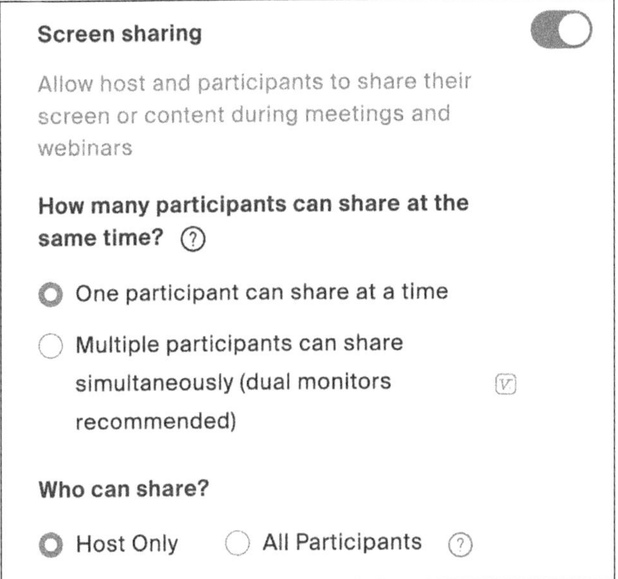

FIGURE 8.4. Confirm that **Host Only** is selected to prevent participants from screen sharing.

Give participants permission to share their screen
"Host Only" means that the host and co-hosts can share their screen. That's one reason I recommend making every speaker a co-host. If you're in a one-on-one or small group meeting and want to give any participant the ability to share their screen, click on the **Security** button at the bottom of the Zoom window and click **Share Screen** to add a checkmark.

Annotation - ✓ Only User Sharing

Enabling this setting prevents purposeful or accidental drawings on shared screens.[7]

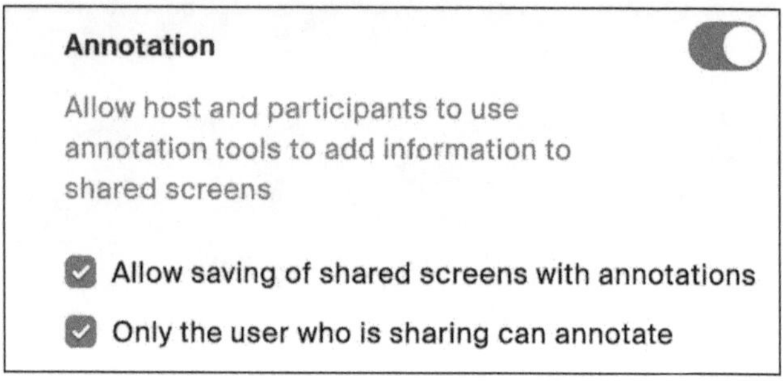

FIGURE 8.5. ✓ **Only the user who is sharing can annotate** to prevent unwanted marks on shared screens.

Give participants the ability to annotate
Want to give participants access to this feature after you've shared your screen? Click **More** on the floating toolbar and select **Annotate**.[8]

Allow Removed Participants to Rejoin

This option should NOT be enabled, or participants you remove from your meeting for being disruptive can easily rejoin.

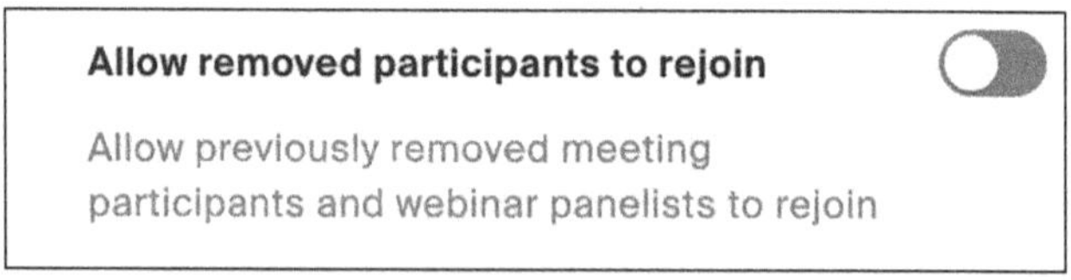

FIGURE 8.6. Ensure that this setting is NOT enabled so removed participants cannot rejoin.

Accidentally removed a participant?

If you accidentally remove someone who should be allowed to rejoin the meeting, you can enable this setting to allow them to rejoin, but it won't take effect until you restart your meeting.[9]

IN MEETING SECURITY SETTINGS

Participants Cannot Unmute

Concerned that a participant may purposely or accidentally unmute during your presentation? Remove that possibility by taking away their ability to unmute themselves. With **Unmute Themselves** disabled, only hosts and co-hosts can unmute.

I recommend enabling this setting for at least the first 20 minutes of any public meeting with a history of Zoom bombers. In my experience, they will make themselves known well before the 20 minute mark, and will be stymied because you took away their ability to unmute.

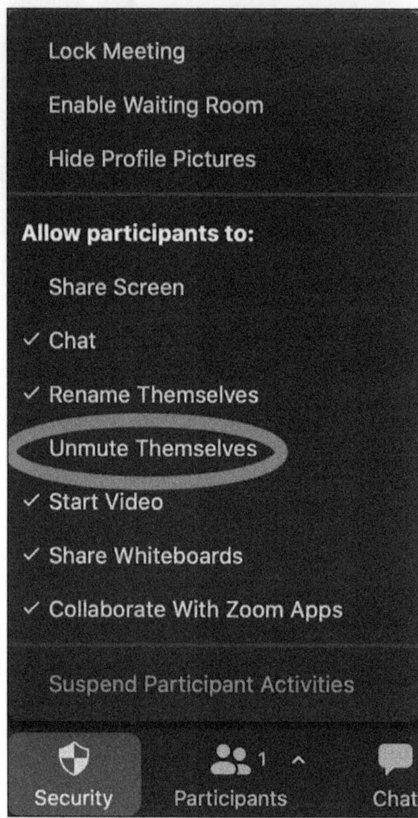

FIGURE 8.7. Click on the **Security** button on the bottom left of the Zoom window and remove the check mark next to **Unmute Themselves.**

Q&A and report back after breakout rooms
Remember to re-enable this setting if you want to allow participants to unmute or click the **Ask to Unmute** button to allow an individual participant to unmute.

FIGURE 8.8. Hover over a participant's video to view the **Ask to Unmute** button on the top right. Click on this button to give any individual participant the ability to unmute when **Unmute Themselves** is disabled on the **Security** button.

Participants Cannot Chat

Open the **Chat** window and click on the **three dots (. . .)** on the bottom. Here are the options:

- Select **No one**—I don't recommend disabling the ability to chat. That creates the opposite of an engaging event. It also means participants cannot communicate tech issues.

- Select **Host and co-hosts**—Participants may send messages to the host and co-hosts, not to everyone or directly to each other.

- Select **Everyone**—Participants may send messages to everyone in the meeting, but not directly to individual participants.

- Select **Everyone and anyone directly**—Generally, this is my recommendation, but there are scenarios where it would be better to disable direct messages, or only have participants message the host and co-hosts.

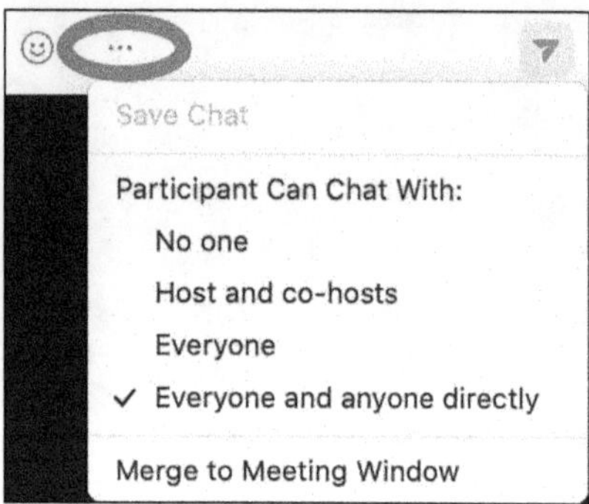

FIGURE 8.9. Click the **three dots (. . .)** at the bottom of the **Chat** window to find these options.

HANDLING ZOOM BOMBERS

As I was writing this chapter, I hosted my monthly #NoMoreBadZoom Virtual Happy Hour.[10] For the first time ever, we had a multi-prong Zoom bombing. Eight of the 38 participants logged on with the intent to be disruptive. I'm proud to say that not a single one was able to unmute or share their screen, and I was generally able to continue the event as planned. I purposely schedule the first breakout room to start 20 minutes into the meeting, because from experience I know that Zoom bombers won't have the patience to wait that long before making themselves known.

When they realized I wasn't going to let them unmute, each one tried to get my attention in their own way. They raised their Zoom hand and then started waving their actual hands in the air. One was standing on a chair. It was all very silly and childish stuff, which makes sense as they were all teenagers. In this case, it was easy to spot the possible problem participants. The event usually attracts participants over the age of 40, so it's out of the norm to have participants clearly under the age of 25 join us.

I removed and reported these participants one by one. I thought I had found them all, but then a participant posted a very off-topic comment in chat to get our attention. I smoothly deleted it and then booted that participant, too. While I would prefer not to have any disruptions, it's so much better to have these settings in place to limit their impact.

The next day, I confirmed each report via the email Zoom sent me, which is how I realized it had been eight in total.

If you host public Zoom events, it's important to know how to quickly remove an individual participant and also how to pull the "In case of emergency" cord if necessary.

Remove an Individual Participant

You need to be a host or co-host to remove a participant.

If you can see the participant in the **Gallery View**, hover your mouse over their video and click on the **three dots** (. . .) on the top right, and then select **Remove** or **Report**. Doing so will remove the partici-pant. You will receive an email asking you to confirm the report within seven days. If you do, the report is sent to the Zoom Trust and Safety team. They will determine if there was a misuse of the platform and, if so, block the user.[11]

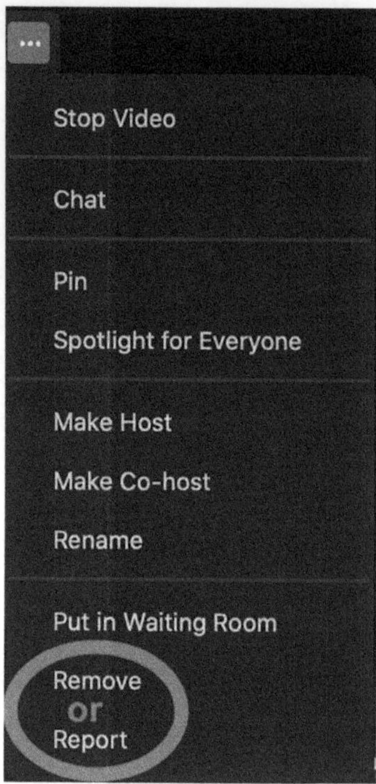

FIGURE 8.10. Click on the **three dots (. . .)** at the top right of a participant's video and then select **Remove** or **Report**.

*In my experience, clicking **Remove** or **Report** results in the same outcome. The participant is removed from the Zoom meeting, and I receive an email asking me to confirm the report within seven days. So don't stress about which one you click on in the moment.*

If you can't see the person but you know their name (e.g., they're posting off-color comments in chat), locate them in the **Participant** list, hover your cursor over their name, click the **More** button, click

Remove or **Report**.[12] This is another reason to always have the **Participant** list window open when you are presenting or hosting.

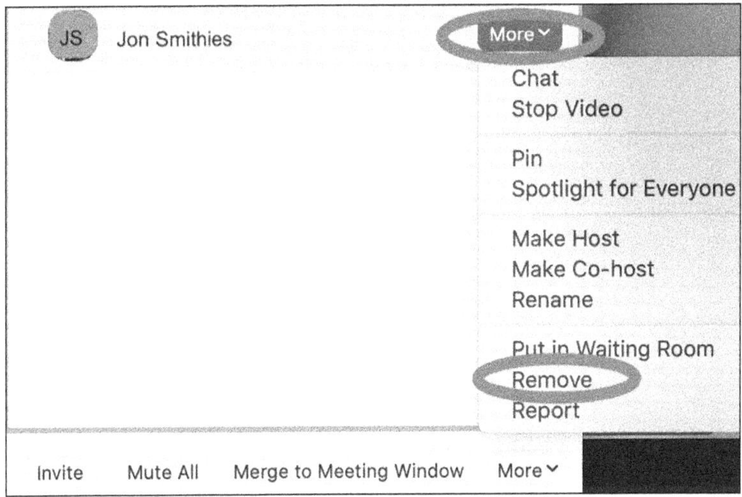

FIGURE 8.11. In the **Participant** window, click the **More** button next to a participant's name to find this menu and then select **Remove** or **Report**.

With a little bit of practice, this can be done smoothly. The difficult part is deciding what rises to the level of disruption that warrants removal, and not accidentally removing someone who was not in the wrong. Remember, based on the settings listed above, someone removed cannot rejoin that Zoom link.

If this meeting used a registration page for a recurring meeting, make sure you cancel registration for anyone you removed. Otherwise, they will receive the confirmation email sent for the next meeting.

Pull in Case of Emergency

What I'm about to describe is about as subtle as breaking glass and pulling the brake on a moving train. In other words, you better have a really good reason for doing it. You'll need to know the steps to get the train, er meeting, back on track.

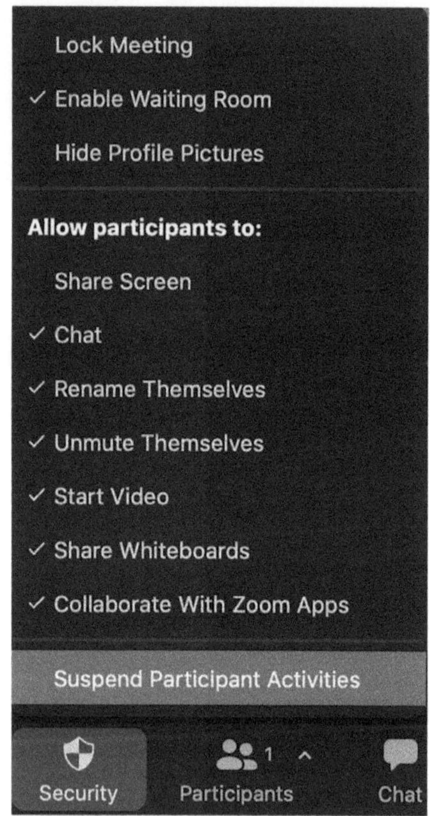

FIGURE 8.12. If you click **Suspend Participant Activities** *everything* stops.

This feature is called **Suspend Participant Activities**.[13] When you activate it, everything on Zoom will stop. Everyone will be muted. Cameras are off. Profile photos are removed. Shared screen is stopped.

Breakout rooms are closed. Chat is disabled. The waiting room is enabled. The meeting will be locked, so no one can join—even when the waiting room is disabled.

Your camera and microphone will also be turned off, so for a moment everyone will be plunged into silence and wonder what's going on. I'll walk you through how to initiate this feature and how to handle the aftermath.

To start:

- Click on the **Security** badge button on the bottom left of the Zoom window.

- Click on **Suspend Participant Activities**.

- Only practicing? **Uncheck Report** to Zoom.

- Click **Suspend** button.

- Now everyone's video is black, with just their names showing.

- Unmute yourself and turn your camera back on so everyone can see you and know you're in control of the situation.

- Explain to everyone that you're handling the intrusion and to give you a moment.

- A list of participants will appear before you, giving you the ability to remove any one of them, or more than one, if necessary.

- Find the people who are causing problems and remove them. (If only one or two people, see above for the more subtle way to remove individual participants.)

To continue the meeting, click on the **Security** badge again.

- Click on **Start Video** and let participants know they can turn their cameras back on.

- Click on **Chat** so participants can use that feature again.

- Click on **Hide Profile Pictures** to remove the checkmark, so anyone who keeps their camera off will show their profile image.

- Click on **Lock Meeting,** in case someone loses access to the internet and needs to rejoin your room.

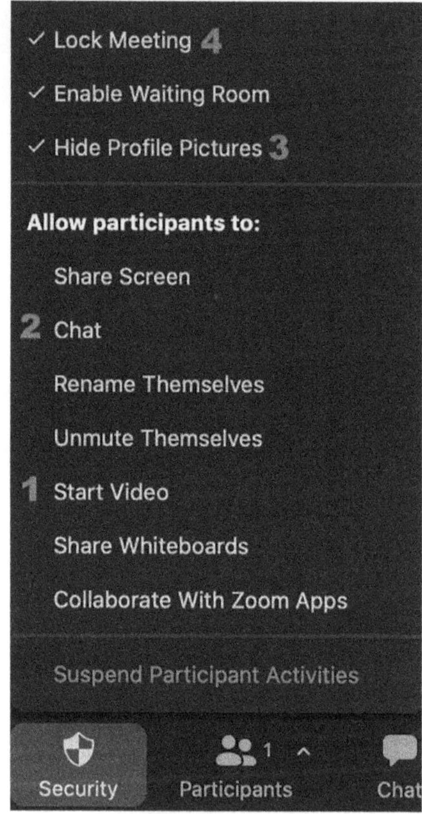

FIGURE 8.13. Starting at the bottom of the **Security** list, click on **Start Video**, **Chat**, **Hide Profile Pictures**, and **Lock Meeting**.

Let participants know you've taken care of the problem and will continue with the agenda. By keeping the **Waiting Room** enabled, you can individually admit anyone who tries to join from this point on.

If you do any kind of report back or other activity that invites participants to speak, remember that participants are still unable to unmute
until you check **Unmute Themselves** on the **Security** badge button.

OTHER POTENTIAL RISKS

No Internet

*What would you do if the morning of your big virtual event you woke up
to discover your home or office does not have internet?*

Investigate getting redundant internet. This means you pay for two internet service providers. Make sure they're using different technology
(e.g., cable vs. fiber optic) because cable companies piggyback on each
other's cables. If one is down, they likely all are. Consider this an insur-
ance policy. If you're at home, this also allows you to be the exclusive
user of one service, while your family uses the other service for all of
their devices. No more sharing bandwidth during important calls.

*My assistant was able to negotiate a reduced monthly
fee for her redundant internet service provider. She
pays a small monthly fee and only pays more if she
uses the service.*

No Electricity

What if you have no electricity?

Do you know another location to which you can drive quickly to access the internet? Is there a co-working space that sells day passes? A
friend with an empty office to offer? No? Is your phone fully charged?

Can you use it as an internet hot spot? Do you have the Zoom link and call-in number saved to your online calendar for easy access? Does someone else have your slide deck file so they can share it for you? Do you have your slides and notes printed out, so you can call in and present with audio only while someone else shares your slides?

Sharing Video

Are you relying on poor quality internet to share a critically important video from YouTube?

To send a file from YouTube, you need Zoom to download and upload very quickly. If you're experiencing internet issues, that will result in a poor quality video. Download the file to your computer to share from your desktop to minimize technical issues.

Computer Updates

Is your computer due for updates?

Restart your computer the day before, so you're not impatiently waiting for the updates to complete when you're minutes away from the start of the event.

Keeping your events safe from intrusion is about minimizing risk. Follow the steps in this chapter and you'll be prepared with the right settings and the knowledge of how to use those settings to thwart anyone trying to disrupt your meeting. Practice the steps in this chapter with friends before your next virtual event, so you're ready to take action.

CHAPTER NINE

Settings

Why, hello there! If you're here, you're ready to update all your Zoom settings, or perhaps there's a specific Zoom feature you're missing? It's your choice. You can go step-by-step through this chapter to enable ALL the settings I recommend, or you can skip ahead to the section that will help you enable a specific feature.

You're probably thinking, "I'll just skip ahead then." Before you do, consider that by reading through the entire chapter, you may discover new features and options that you didn't even know existed. That's why I recommend you keep reading as I walk you through all the options.

Just reading this chapter will give you a new appreciation for all that Zoom can do for you. Without further delay, let's dig in.

ACCOUNT, PROFILE, AND DESKTOP CLIENT SETTINGS

Where are the settings located? There are a few answers to that question.

- Account Settings are on www.Zoom.us. Only an account administrator can edit these settings. (Note: if you have a Zoom Pro account, you are the administrator.)[1]

- Profile Settings are on www.Zoom.us.[2]

- Desktop client-level settings (a.k.a. app settings) are on your computer.[3]

Account Settings

If you have a Zoom Pro account, it's unlikely that you'll ever need to adjust the Account Settings on your Zoom account. It's helpful to know this exists if you try to make an account-level change that requires an administrator's permission (which you can provide since you're the admin).

To access your Zoom Account Settings, log into your account at www. Zoom.us. On the left side of the screen, there's a menu. Scroll down until you see **Account Management**. Click that and then select **Account Settings**. If you're familiar with Profile Settings, the page will look similar, but some settings are only available on this page.

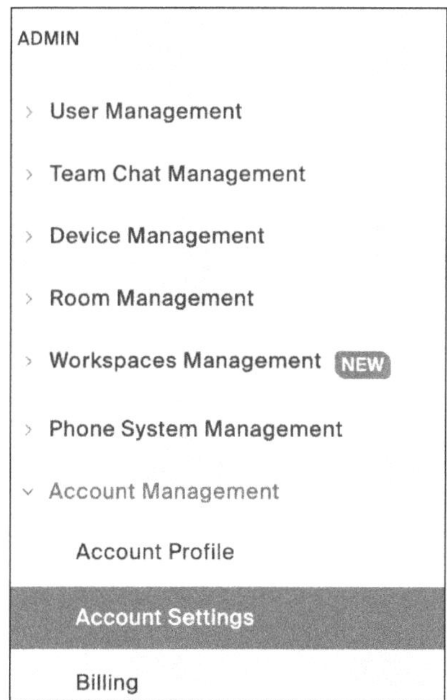

FIGURE 9.1. This is the menu on the bottom left side of your screen after you log in at www.Zoom.us.

Profile Settings

This is where users enable all the settings available to them that are not on by default (e.g., breakout rooms and captions).

To access your Zoom Profile Settings, log into your account at www. Zoom.us. On the left side of the screen is a menu where you'll find **Settings**. Click on that option, and the right side of the screen will display **Meeting** settings (next to this is the **Recording** settings, which I'll also address in this chapter).

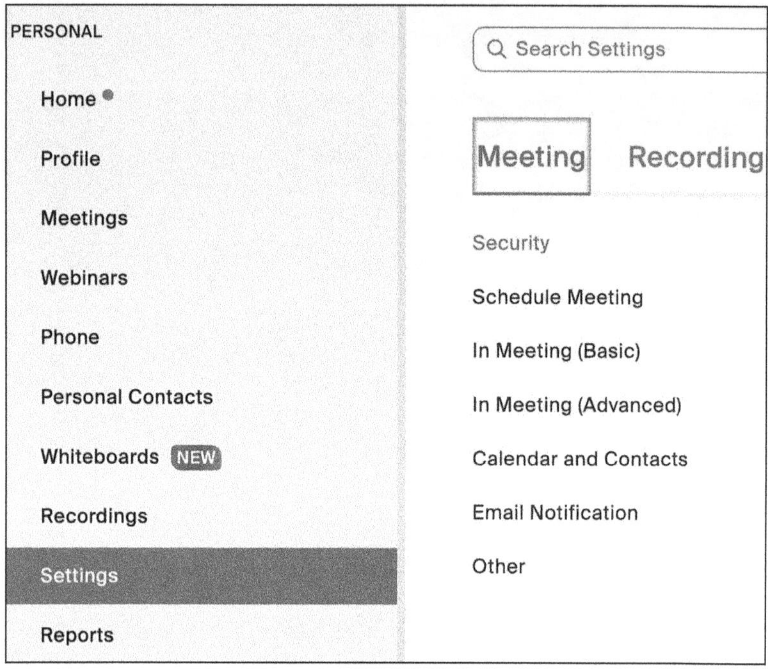

FIGURE 9.2. This is the menu on the left side of your screen after you log in at www.Zoom.us.

What you see on the **Meetings** settings page depends on whether the Zoom account is licensed (Pro, Business, or Enterprise) or a free (Basic) account. If you don't have a licensed account, you may wonder what features you're missing and whether it's worth paying for Zoom. (The short answer is yes! It's worth the $149.99 annual fee.[4] If you're using Zoom as a professional or in your business, you should have access to all of Zoom's features.)

The following features are available for everyone but need to be enabled. The **#NoMoreBadZoom Settings Checklist** is organized in the order of appearance. You can also use the search bar at the top of the page to quickly locate each one.

While I'm not explaining why I recommend these settings, know that they must be enabled to access the features described in this book.

If you're a Zoom user connected to a Business or Enterprise account, you may find some **Meeting** setting options are restricted on your account. If this happens, you'll need to contact your Zoom account administrator.

Table 9.1 #NoMoreBadZoom Settings Checklist

✓	Waiting Room
✓	Host + Participants Video On
✓	Mute all participants when they join
✓	New meeting chat experience
✓	Always show meeting control toolbar
✓	Annotation: ✓ **Only user sharing**
✓	Non-verbal feedback
✓	Breakout room: ✓ **Broadcast message to participants**
✓	Automated captions
✓	Full transcript
✓	Save captions (optional)
✓	Show a Join from your browser link
✓	Request permission to unmute

These features are only available for a licensed account (Pro, Business, or Enterprise):	
✓	Customize Waiting Room
✓	Allow Co-host
✓	Polls + Advanced Polls
✓	Allow livestreaming of meetings
✓	Meeting Survey
✓	Language Interpretation
✓	Group HD video
Aside from these settings, there are additional benefits of having a licensed account:	
✓	Host meetings over forty minutes
✓	Meeting templates (including polls)
✓	Set up a registration form
✓	Record to the Zoom cloud
✓	Upgrade to large meetings and webinar

Want to save this for easy reference or pass this along to a client or colleague? Download the #NoMoreBadZoom Settings Checklist PDF at www.robbiesamuels.com/breakout.

Update Your Name

When you're in a meeting, you can update your Zoom name. You may want to use a nickname, only your first name, add your kids' ages if you're attending a parent social, or share your location.

There are a few ways to do this after you've been let into the meeting (it's not possible when you're in the waiting room).

- Hover your cursor over your video and click on the **three dots** (...) that appear in the top right corner, then select **Rename** from the menu that appears.

- On a Mac, click on your video to bring up that menu and then click **Rename**.

- On a PC, right-click on your video to bring up that menu and then click **Rename**.

- Click on the Participants button on the bottom left of your Zoom window. In the Participants window that appears, hover over your name and click on the **More** button. Then select Rename.[5]

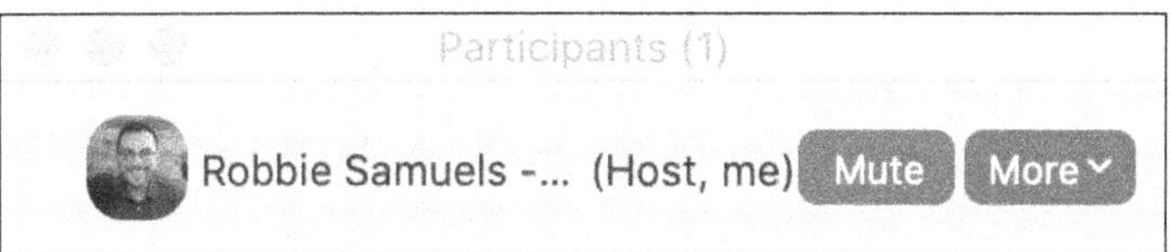

FIGURE 9.3. Locate your name in the **Participant** window and select the **More** button to Rename.

Are you tired of having to add your organization name, location, and/or pronouns every time you join a Zoom meeting? There's a way to reduce the number of times you'll have to do that. Use **Display Name**—an option in the **Profile** section of <u>Zoom.us</u>.[6]

Log into your account and click on **Profile** on the top of the left menu. Then click **Edit** on the right side of the next screen.

Type into the **Display Name** field what you'd like to show when you join Zoom. You can incorporate your pronouns into this field—for example, Robbie Samuels - (he/him) Philadelphia, PA USA.

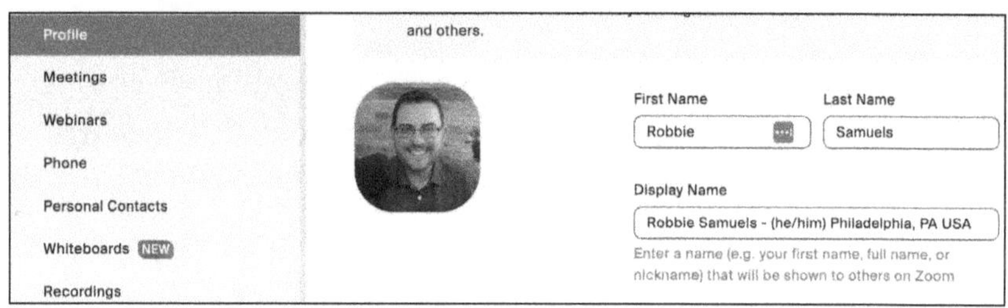

FIGURE 9.4. Select **Profile** on the left menu to edit your **Display Name**.

Another option for pronouns is to add them in the **Pronouns** field and select **Always share** or **Ask me**. This option will place your pronouns after whatever you wrote in the **Display Name** field.

*Even after updating the **Display Name**, there are some meetings you'll join where you'll notice that only your first and last name will be visible. Why? It's because those meetings used a Zoom registration page. Only what you wrote in the first and last name field on the registration form will be your Zoom name. A workaround is to add a dash after your last name and add your organization. Another reason this may not work is if you're not logged into Zoom on that device. Locate the Zoom desktop client (the app) and enter your login credentials.[7]*

PRONOUNS?

If you've never had anyone question your gender, it may seem like knowing whether to say he or she to refer to a person is fairly obvious. Unfortunately, we tend to identify a person's gender based on assumptions that aren't always accurate, and sometimes we guess wrong. Using assumptions to determine a person's gender also reinforces the idea that looking a certain way is required to be perceived as a specific gender, so it's a harmful practice even when we guess correctly.

Inviting all participants to share pronouns creates space for participants who may use a pronoun that might not be assumed correctly. When a transgender participant (someone whose gender does not match the sex assigned at birth) gets to share their pronouns, they will be accurately identified during your meeting. A cisgender participant (someone whose gender matches the sex assigned at birth) sharing pronouns is an act of solidarity and allyship. Learn more at http://pronouns.org.

Desktop Client Settings

As I mentioned earlier, some of the settings you'll need to adjust are on your Zoom desktop client (a.k.a. your computer's app). To access these settings, join a Zoom meeting and look at the bottom left of your Zoom window. Next, click on the ^ to the right of **Stop/Start Video** and then click on **Video Settings**.

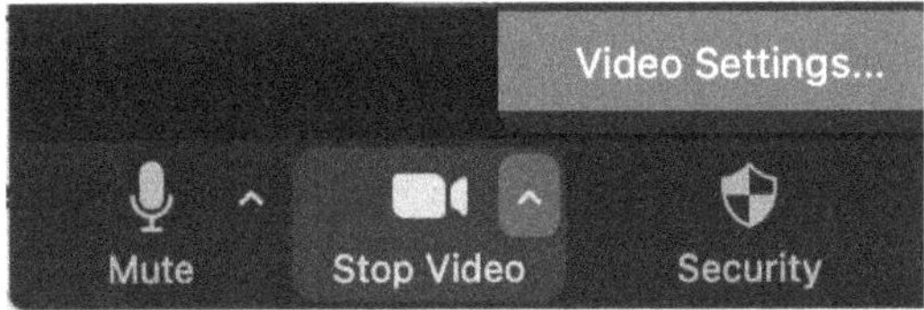

FIGURE 9.5. Next to the Stop Video button, in the lower-left corner of the Zoom window, is an up arrow. Click on that to select Video Settings.

A pop-up window will appear with a menu on the left side of the screen. I will walk you through all of these options, starting with **General**. I'll share my recommendations for what to select, but you may want to make different choices now that you know where these settings exist.

To streamline this checklist, I'll skip over settings I don't universally rec-ommend. **Unless I specify "uncheck," I recommend you check the box.**

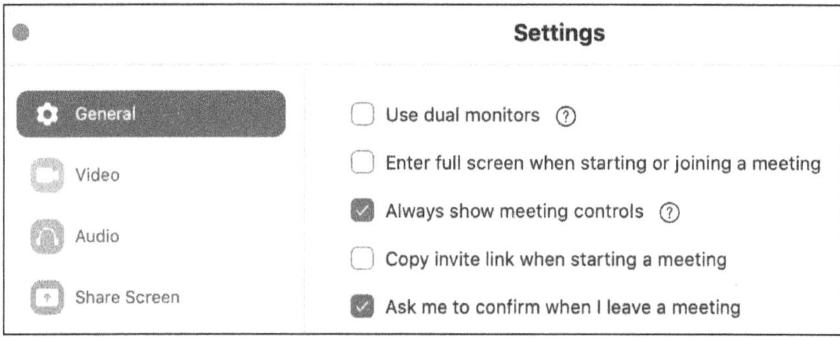

Figure 9.6. On the screen that appears after clicking on Video Settings, select **General** from the left menu.

General

Click on **General** on the top left. On the right side of the next screen:

- *Uncheck* Enter full screen when starting or joining a meeting
  If you've ever clicked a link in the chat and lost your Zoom window, the reason is that your Zoom was full screen. There are two options to change—this one and one listed under **Share Screen**.

- Always show meeting controls
  This is the Zoom toolbar at the bottom of your Zoom window. It's much faster to navigate to record, launch polls, etc., if the toolbar is already showing.

- Ask me to confirm when I leave a meeting
Avoid accidentally leaving a meeting by clicking the wrong button.

- Show meeting timers
A clock showing the duration of the Zoom meeting will appear on the top right of the Zoom window. It's easier to glance at this than at your computer clock when in a meeting.

- Show profile icon next to in meeting chat messages
This requires that you've already uploaded a profile image. If you haven't done this yet, visit Zoom.us, click on Profile, and then edit to add an image.

- Automatically keep Zoom desktop client up to date
*Highly recommended. You choose whether to update **Fast** (newest features and updates) or **Slow** (fewer updates, better stability), but without this checked, your Zoom will become out of date very quickly.[8]*

Scroll to the bottom of this page to find the following options:

- Skin tone
The default is yellow, but if you don't want to look like a Simpson family member, choose from a range of skin tones.

- Activate the following emojis based on hand gesture recognition
This allows you to gesture to raise your Zoom hand or give a thumbs up.

*If you're looking for a quick way to raise your Zoom hand, try **Alt + Y** on a PC or **Option + Y** on a Mac.*

- Display your reactions above toolbar
  Reminds you that you have your Zoom hand raised and gives you a quick way to lower it.

- Animate these emojis
  This new feature is on by default, but you can toggle it off here.

Video

- Original Ratio
  Only check/uncheck this if you see black bars on either side of your video while logged in on a computer. This may fix that problem.

- HD
  It's not necessary to turn this on. While it may make you look better, it will also take up more bandwidth and create larger video files.

- Mirror my video
  This will ONLY change the way YOU view your video. If you'd like to learn more, go to Chapter Four of this book and read The Future is Left — Mirroring Online *section, where I explain in-depth about how this feature works.*

- Touch up my appearance
  Blurs your image a smidge to hide blemishes. Be careful, though, as going too far to the right looks unnatural.

- Always display participant name on their videos
  Very helpful when facilitating, as you no longer have to hover your cursor over someone's video to view their name.

- Hide non-video participants

Hide non-video participants
If there are only two participants in a Zoom meeting, it's not possible to use the **Spotlight** feature. If you need to record a speaker without your video or profile picture showing on the recording, check this box and turn off your camera. Voila! Your voice will be recorded if you unmute, but your profile picture will not be on the recording.

- Hide Self View
  Select if you'd prefer not to look at your own video. This option also appears on the menu you can access by clicking on your own video while in a Zoom meeting.

- Maximum participants displayed per screen in Gallery View:
  If your device meets CPU requirements, you'll see an option to display up to forty-nine participants.[9]

Audio

- Speaker
  Use this to choose an audio output source.

- Microphone
  Switch and test your microphone input.

- Automatically adjust microphone volume
  Recommended, although if your volume is too low, change this setting and manually move input volume to the right.

- Background noise suppression
  *Switch from **Auto** to **High** to minimize background noise (e.g., dogs or your neighbor's lawn mower) if you're not using a microphone that suppresses background noise. Enabling this may increase CPU output on your device.*

Scroll down for additional options

- Automatically join computer audio when joining a meeting
  *With this checked, you'll no longer have to select computer audio
  vs. phone audio each time you join a meeting.*

- Mute my mic when joining a meeting
  *Use this if you find yourself joining meetings that don't have
  all participants muted upon entry, and you don't want to
  accidentally interrupt.*

- Press and hold Space Key to temporarily unmute
  *Allows you to quickly unmute, but it only works if your cursor
  is clicked on the Zoom meeting (e.g., if your cursor is in email or
  another window, it won't work).*

- Sync buttons on headset
  *This is handy if you have a mute button option on your headset
  and have to remember to double unmute.*

Share Screen

- Window size when screen sharing: **Maintain current size**
  *You need to adjust this second option to stop Zoom from going
  full screen. In this case, it will stop Zoom from going full screen
  when someone shares their screen. The other option is under
  General.*

- Scale to fit shared content to Zoom window
  Adjusts to the size of your Zoom window.

- Show my Zoom Windows to other participants when I am
  screen sharing
  *Not seeing this option? If you're teaching someone how to use
  Zoom, you'll need to enable this at <u>Zoom.us</u> before it becomes an*

option on the desktop client settings. With this turned on, you can show your desktop client windows when sharing your desktop.

- Side-by-side Mode
Places the speaker video to the right of shared content when someone else shares their screen.

Background & Effects

- Virtual Backgrounds
If you want to upload additional virtual backgrounds, click on the + on the top right. Read Chapter Two's Virtual Background Dos & Don'ts *section to learn my best practices and what to avoid when selecting a virtual background.*

- Video Filters
Generally, these are for fun and not appropriate for presentations.

Add custom video filters

It's not obvious how to add custom video filters, but it is possible. Doing so allows you to have screen overlays without using third-party video production tools (e.g., OBS[10] or Ecamm Live).[11] Watch my Custom Video Filters Tutorial and download other resources at www.robbiesamuels.com/breakout.

- Avatars
This feature allows you to design your own avatar. If you need to be off camera but want to show you're engaged during a meeting, this could be an option.

Recording

- Store my recordings at:
  *By default, computer recordings are saved in the **Documents** folder in a **Zoom** folder. If you want to change this default, you could have recordings saved to a cloud folder (e.g., Google Drive, Box, or Dropbox) or to another local folder on your computer.*

- Choose a location to save the recording after the meeting ends
  You can leave the default and still select a different file folder for some recordings.

- Record a separate audio file of each participant
  This is important if you're repurposing the audio for a podcast, as it makes it easier for an editor to even out each speaker's audio levels and remove background noise.

- Optimize for 3rd party video editor
  Not recommended, unless you'll be sending recording files to an editor, as the file size will be increased, and it will take longer to render.

- Record video during screen sharing:
  If you plan to share your screen and your camera video simultaneously, you must enable this. If you don't enable this, your camera video will not show up in the final recording. Note: The recording will be more engaging if you include the shared screen and your camera video.

- Place video next to the shared screen in the recording:
  *If you enable this, in the final recording, your camera video will appear centered in black, to the right of whatever you share on your screen. If you share full screen slides, for example, this means the speaker video won't cover any part of your slides when you record on **your computer**.*

- Cloud Recording
*Additional cloud recording settings are available at **Zoom.us Settings**.[12] See the* Recording Options & Settings *section of this chapter for more information.*

Are participants accidentally showing up in the recording? If you're BOTH recording to your computer and sharing your screen, the computer recording will show six videos stacked vertically on the right side of the screen and will partially cover the shared screen in the recording. To avoid this, record to the cloud using the setting: **Record active speaker with shared screen**. Other options are to have someone else record to their computer or share their screen while you record to your computer.

Profile

Edit My Profile brings you to the **Profile** section of Zoom.us, where you can update your **Display Name** and add your pronouns.

View Advanced Features brings you to the **Settings** section of Zoom.us.

Feedback

If you have suggestions for Zoom, submit them here. If you have technical questions, sign in at https://support.zoom.us/hc/en-us.

- **Chatbot** is available for all Zoom accounts.

- **Submit web tickets** is only available for licensed users.

- **Live chat support** is available for subscription plans greater than $50 USD/month.

Keyboard Shortcuts

*My favorite is to use **Alt + Y (Option + Y)** to Raise and Lower Hand.*

Accessibility

- Adjust the size of the closed captioning font and increase/ decrease the size of the font in **Chat**.

- Automatically dim video when flashing images or visual patterns (such as stripes) are detected.

- If you use a screen reader, this is where you can enable/disable various options.

> ***Increase Chat Font Size***
>
> *Did you know you can increase the font size for chat? This is a game-changer. The default font is tiny, but you can increase it to 120% or higher. On a PC, put your cursor in the **chat** comments box and click **CTRL** and the +/= button. On a Mac, click **CMD** and the +/= button. Toggle the size up and down using the + and - buttons on your keyboard. Once set, this will be the default size for your **chat** window.*

RECORDING OPTIONS & SETTINGS

If you have a licensed Zoom account (Pro, Business, or Enterprise), you have the option to record either to the Zoom cloud or to your computer. If you have a Basic (free) account, you don't have the ability to record to the cloud. If you're the host and on a mobile device (e.g., iPhone, Android, iPad), you may only record to the cloud.

The format of the replay video differs, depending on whether you record to the cloud or the computer and what settings you select. Experiment with the following options to see what you prefer.

Trying to decide which view you prefer?
Record to the cloud AND to your computer by giving your Zoom producer or any other participant the ability to record to their computer. To do this, click on the **three dots (. . .)** on the top right of their video thumbnail once you've started a Zoom meeting and select **Allow to Record Local Files**.

Record on this Computer

By default, these files are saved in a **Documents** folder in a folder named **Zoom**:

PC: C:\Users\User Name\Documents\Zoom

or

Mac: /Users/User Name/Documents/Zoom

Change the default folder
There is an option to change this setting and have the recording save to a different cloud service (Google Drive, Box, Dropbox) or another location on your computer.

There are a few things you should know about how the replay will look when you record to your computer:

- The recording does *not* follow the spotlight (even though it used to!). This means that if you're recording a speaker in the spotlight, and you switch to **Gallery View** to see how participants are responding, the recording will show the **Gallery View** until you switch back to **Speaker View**.

FIGURE 9.7. Even if you spotlight a speaker, if you switch to Gallery View while recording to your computer you will see participants, not just the speaker on the recording.[13]

- If you're BOTH recording to your computer AND sharing your screen, the computer recording will show the speaker's video and five other participant videos. To avoid this, record to the cloud using the setting: **Record active speaker with shared screen**. Other options are to have someone else record to their computer or have someone else share their screen while you record to your computer.

- If you add a second spotlight, the computer recording *will* show both videos on the screen side-by-side. You may spotlight up to nine participants, and they'll all appear on the replay video. (The cloud recording only shows one speaker at a time when two or more are in the spotlight.)

- See the *Desktop Client Settings* section in this chapter to learn how to avoid having the speaker video cover the top right corner of the slide when the speaker shares their screen. If you don't make this adjustment, the slides should be designed with no content on the top right corner.

- If no one is in the spotlight when the speaker shares their screen (i.e., you're seeing the **Gallery View**), then the computer recording will show six videos stacked vertically on the right side of the screen, possibly covering the shared content (see the above point).

- See the *Desktop Client Settings* section in this chapter to enable side-by-side mode before recording to the computer. Then adjust the screen by moving the divider so the speaker video takes up *half the screen*. The video recording will show a larger video for the speaker on the right side of the slide. If the slider is too far to the right, the speaker video on the recording will be *very tiny*. Practice this by recording with the divider in different locations and watch the replay to see what you prefer.

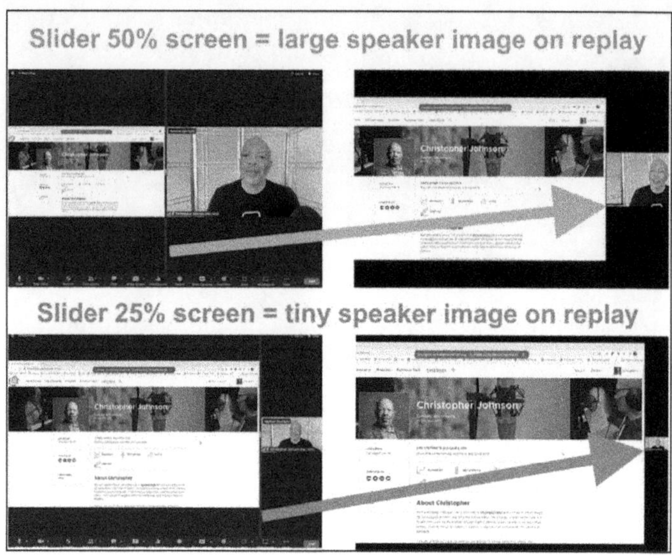

FIGURE 9.8. Adjust the side-by-side slider, so the speaker's video fills half the screen. Then the recording will show a larger speaker video. Too far to the right and the speaker video will be much smaller.

Because you can spotlight more than one person when recording to a computer, the viewing experience may be less jarring than a cloud recording when spotlighting multiple people (e.g., an interview or panel). The cloud recording automatically switches the speaker video each time anyone makes a noise.

Record to the Cloud

Home

Profile

Meetings

Webinars

Phone

Personal Contacts

Whiteboards (NEW)

Recordings

Settings

Reports

Meeting   Recording

Recording

Local recording

Allow hosts and participants to
shared content with user's own

☑ Save chat messages from

☑ Save closed caption as a V

Advanced local recording set

☑ Hosts can give meeting pa

FIGURE 9.9. To access the replay, log into <u>Zoom.us</u> and click on
Recordings on the left side menu. There are several settings to choose for
cloud recordings. To find these, log in at <u>Zoom.us</u> and select **Settings** from
the left menu. The **Recording** settings are at the top middle of the screen,
to the right of **Meeting**.

If you don't have unlimited cloud storage, which is only available to
Enterprise users, you may need to be selective about which options you
check to reduce the number of files saved to the cloud. I've checked the
minimum options I recommend below.[14]

✓ Record active speaker with shared screen.
*Zoom says that the speaker video will be to the right of the shared
content. In my experience, the speaker video appears in the top
right corner of the shared content. For this reason, if you record to
the cloud, it's important that you design your slides so no content
appears in the top right corner.*

☐ Record gallery view with shared screen.
The speaker video and five participant videos will be visible to the right of the shared content. In my experience, this may include participants who are not in the spotlight, so use with caution.

☐ Record active speaker, gallery view and shared screen separately.
If you're going to edit the video, this gives you the most options for what you want to splice together. (If applicable, see the Optimize the recording for 3rd Party video editor setting in the Advanced Cloud Recording Settings section below.)

✓ Record audio-only files.

✓ Record one audio file for all participants.
If one person has background noise, it's more difficult to edit that out if you only have one audio file for everyone who spoke.

☐ Record a separate audio file of each participant.
Useful if you're working with an audio engineer (e.g., for a podcast) or a video editor.

✓ Save chat messages from the meeting / webinar.

Advanced Cloud Recording Settings

☐ Add a timestamp to the recording.
Useful if you want to embed the date and time into the video.

☐ Display participants' names in the recording.

✓ Record thumbnails when sharing.
Display the speaker video when they share their screen.

☐ Optimize the recording for 3rd party video editor.
This ensures compatibility with video editing software, although it does increase the file size.

☐ Save panelist chat to the recording.

Only relates to webinar. Be cautious, as it includes messages sent to panelists that you may not want to be public.

✓ Save poll results shared during the meeting/webinar.
Helpful if you want to be able to share poll results, since the poll does not show on the video recording.

✓ Save closed caption as a VTT file.
Useful if you want to embed captions in your video.

You can manage your cloud storage by deleting recordings you no longer need or that you have already downloaded to your computer or to a different cloud storage (such as Dropbox, Box, or Google Drive).[15] Another option is to purchase additional cloud storage (e.g., 30 GB for $10/month, 200 GB for $40, month).[16]

"This Meeting is Being Recorded."

Have you ever had a speaker thrown off by the announcement that the meeting is being recorded? They were just introduced, and as they begin speaking, a voice declares: *This meeting is being recorded.*[17]

While that is NOT heard on the replay, it often throws off the speaker, and they start over a bit flustered. There are a couple of ways to prevent that from happening.

One option is to either set the recording to happen automatically or hit record as soon as you enter the Zoom meeting. If you're sharing the replay video, plan to trim the video, so replay viewers only see the meeting from the opening speaker.

Participants will still see a pop-up button letting them know that the meeting is being recorded and requiring them to accept it before they turn on their cameras or unmute.

> *Another option is you can turn off the announcement! It's true. Zoom set this up as a default, but you can go to the **Recording** settings at <u>Zoom.us</u> and scroll to the bottom of the page to the **Play voice prompt for** section and move the radio button to: **No one**.*

Recording notifications - Zoom clients ⓘ

Play voice prompt for

○ All participants   ○ Guest only   ⑦   ⦿ No one

FIGURE 9.10. Turn off the announcement: "This meeting is being recorded." Scroll down to the bottom of cloud recording settings and select **No one** for Recording notifications – Zoom clients.

The benefit of this option is that you can hit **Record** right as the meeting's program is underway. This means you won't need to edit the replay recording and can share that file without delay.

Record Automatically

This is an option you can check when scheduling your Zoom meeting. Download my Scheduling Zoom Meeting Guide PDF at <u>www.robbiesamuels.com/breakout</u>.

UPDATE ZOOM

Are you on Zoom all the time? Is it a lifeline in your business? Have you been regularly updating Zoom so you always have a recent version on your computer?

No? Well, there's good news and bad news.

The bad news is that you're missing out on the latest features if you don't update regularly. Often, these features will be very helpful for your virtual presentations.

The good news is that it's easier than ever to stay current. There's an option to select **Automatically** to keep your Zoom desktop client (a.k.a. your computer app) up to date.

1. Launch a Zoom meeting on your computer.

2. Look at the bottom left corner of the Zoom window.

3. Click on the ^ to the right of the microphone.

4. Select **Audio Settings**.

5. Select **General** at the top of the menu on the left side of the pop-up screen.

6. On the right side of the screen, look for **Zoom Updates**.

7. Check the box and select either **Fast** (newest features and updates) or **Slow** (fewer updates, better stability).[18]

8. When you join a Zoom meeting, you'll be prompted (at the frequency you selected) to update your Zoom desktop client.

In other good news, you'll never again be more than 10 months out of date—even if you skip all of those suggested updates. The Zoom Software Quarterly Lifecycle Policy was instituted in November 2022 when Zoom required every user to update to the 5.8.6 version of the desktop client. It happened again three months later in February 2023, when the minimum version required became 5.10.3.[19]

If something is amiss with Zoom—it was working one day and isn't now—it's likely there was a glitch in the last update you installed. The quickest fix is to uninstall and reinstall the desktop client. First, uninstall the application on your Mac[20] or PC,[21] then download a new desktop client application at www.zoom.us/downloads. Unfortunately, this will remove any images you uploaded as Zoom backgrounds. You will also have to reset your desktop client settings. See *Desktop Client Settings* section in this chapter.

SCHEDULING A MEETING

Some settings you'll need to adjust are available as you schedule a meeting. Are you using your Personal Meeting ID (PMI) for all your Zoom meetings? There are a few reasons I recommend against this. The main one is that if you schedule a non-PMI Zoom link for a group meeting and it's compromised (i.e., your meeting is disrupted by Zoom bombers), you can simply issue a new meeting link for that group. If you use your PMI link for all meetings, you would need to send a new link to everyone who was planning to meet you via your PMI.

Another reason is that you can have different settings for group meetings versus one-on-one meetings. For instance, I use my PMI for one-on-one meetings, and participants are not muted upon entry. When I schedule a group meeting, I don't use my PMI, and I select the setting to mute all participants upon entry. I can also set a recurring meeting, so the same link is used for a particular group every week/month.

What features are you missing if you don't pay for Zoom?
If you have a Basic account (i.e., free), the following features will NOT be available when you schedule a meeting:

- Registration

- Polls/Quizzes

- Survey

- Live Streaming

Steps to Schedule a Meeting:

- Log into www.Zoom.us.

- Click **Schedule** on the top navigation menu.

- What you select next depends on the type of meeting you want to set up. There are three options:

  - One-time meeting

  - Recurring meeting (e.g., weekly or monthly)

  - Meet anytime (no specific date or time)

Are you looking for information about setting up the registration page, polls, survey, or live streaming? You'll find that after this next section.

One-Time Meeting

- Type in the topic.

- Choose when and duration.

- Want to use a registration page? ✓ **Required** (not available for a Basic account).

- Meeting ID: Select **Generate Automatically**.

- Security: ✓ **Passcode** AND **Waiting Room**.

- Video – Host and Participant: Select your preference (I recommend **ON** for both).

- Audio: Select **Both**.

- Options: Click **Show**, then ✓ **Mute participants upon entry**.

- Click **Save** button.

- On the next screen, click **Copy Invitation** button to copy text that includes the Zoom link and phone options. I recommend giving presenters the ability to call in if they experience tech issues. You may also highlight and copy the invite link (or registration link) and share just that with participants.

- Will you need to set up this meeting again? Save it as a template.

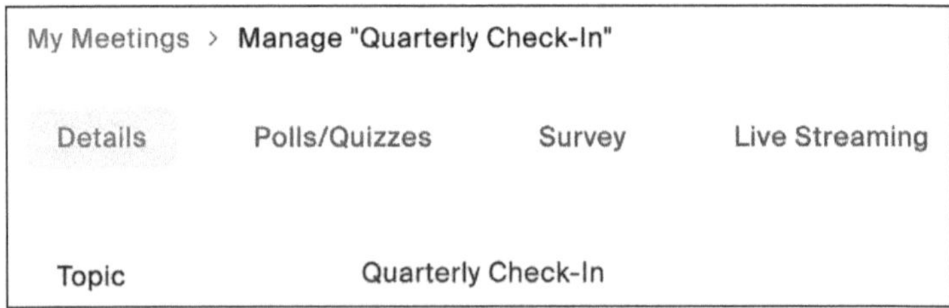

FIGURE 9.11. Want to set up a poll? Go to the top of the Zoom page and select **Polls** (not available for a Basic account).

Recurring Meeting (e.g., Weekly)

- Type in the topic.

- ✓ **Recurring meeting**.

- Recurrence: Select: **Daily, Weekly, Monthly**.

- Repeats every: Select the appropriate time.

- End date: Select the date or number of occurrences.

- Want to use a registration page? ✓ **Required** (not available for a Basic account), then select one of the following options.

  - Attendees register once and can attend any of the occurrences.

  - Attendees need to register for each occurrence to attend.

  - Attendees register once and can choose one or more occurrences to attend.

- Meeting ID: Select **Generate Automatically**.

- Security: ✓ **Passcode** AND **Waiting Room**.

- Video – Host and Participant: Select your preference (I recommend **ON** for both).

- Audio: select **Both**.

- Options: Click **Show**, then ✓ **Mute participants upon entry**.

- Click **Save** button.

- On the next screen, click **Copy Invitation** button to copy text that includes the Zoom link and phone options. I recommend giving presenters the ability to call in if they experience tech issues. You may also highlight and copy the invite link (or registration link) and share just that with participants.

- Want to set up a poll? Go to the top of the Zoom page and select **Polls** (not available for a Basic account).

- Will you need to set up this meeting again? Save it as a template.

Meet Anytime (No Specific Date or Time)

- Type in the topic.

- ✓ **Recurring meeting**.

- Recurrence: Select **No Fixed Time**.

- Registration is not possible if you select **No Fixed Time**.

- Meeting ID: Select **Generate Automatically**.

- Security: ✓ **Passcode** AND **Waiting Room**.

- Video: Host and Participant - select your preference (I recommend **ON** for both).

- Audio: Select **Both**.

- Options: Click **Show**, then ✓ **Mute participants upon entry**.

- Click **Save** button.

- On the next screen, click **Copy Invitation** button to copy text that includes the Zoom link and phone options. I recommend giving presenters the ability to call in if they experience tech issues. You may also highlight and copy the invite link (or registration link) and share just that with participants.

- Want to set up a poll? Go to the top of the Zoom page and select **Polls** (not available for a Basic account).

- Will you need to set up this meeting again? Save it as a template.

POLLS, SURVEYS, LIVE STREAMING

After you save a meeting, you can set up these additional options. If you don't see Polls/Quizzes, Survey, or Live Streaming available, these have not been enabled at **Zoom.us Settings**.[22] Refer back to the first section of this chapter.

Polls or Polls/Quizzes (not available on a Basic account)

- **Create**: Click on the blue button to add a poll.

  Each poll may have one or more questions. If more than one question is added, then participants must answer all of them before hitting submit. If questions should be answered at different points in the presentation, set them up in separate polls.

Advanced polling options

This feature allows participants to type in their answers, select from columns A & B, and more, including quizzes. This must be enabled in **Zoom.us Settings**.[23]

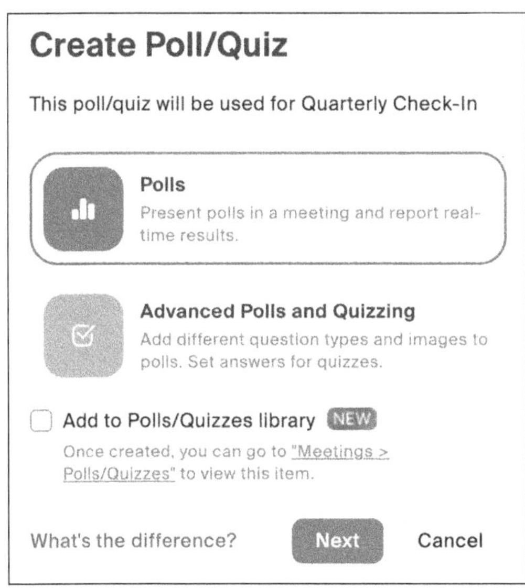

FIGURE 9.12. Enable **Advanced Polls and Quizzes** to have more options when setting up **Polls**.

Survey (not available on a Basic account)

- Create a new survey or use a third-party survey

  Create a new survey means creating a survey (a.k.a. poll) that will appear as participants exit the meeting.

  Use a third-party survey allows you to enter a link to a website that has a survey form. It's possible to enter any website link (e.g., your website), but the language participants see as they exit the meeting will ask if they want to answer a survey. It may confuse participants if they're sent to a website with no survey.

Live streaming (not available on a Basic account)

- Confirm you've already set up the ability to live stream to Facebook, Workplace by Facebook, YouTube, or Twitch.

- Configure **Custom Streaming Service.**

Livestreaming not configured?
Visit **Zoom.us Settings** to enable this feature.[24] This will then be available for all meetings on this Zoom account.

Want to save this for easy reference or pass this along to a client or colleague? Download the #NoMoreBadZoom Scheduling a Meeting PDF and other resources at www. robbiesamuels.com/breakout.

REGISTRATION REQUIRED
(NOT AVAILABLE FOR A BASIC ACCOUNT)

<table>
<tr><td>My Meetings > Manage "Quarterly Check-In"</td></tr>
<tr><td>Details   Registration   Email Settings   Branding   Polls/Quizzes   Survey   Live Streaming</td></tr>
<tr><td>Topic   Quarterly Check-In</td></tr>
</table>

FIGURE 9.13. After you've checked the **Registration Required** box and saved the meeting, go to the top of the meeting page to view registrants, edit confirmation email, add branding, and more.

Registration

- Manage Registrants: Select **View** on the right to see a list of registrants.

  Each participant receives a unique Zoom link to join the meeting. This link can be copied and sent to them by searching for them in this list of registrants.

Need to download the RSVP list?
Download a registration report. I shared the steps to run reports in the Post-Event section of Chapter Six.

- Registration options: Select **Edit** on the right to decide whether to receive an email when someone registers, to close registration after a specific date or number of registrants, etc. At the top of this pop-up, you'll also see **Questions** and **Custom Questions**. Select these to collect additional information on the registration form.

Email Settings

- Select **Email Language.** The default is the recipients' language.

- Email Contact: This will default to the email address on the Zoom account but can be updated.

- Confirmation Email to Registrations: Select **Edit** on the right to update the email subject line and message.

Where's the Zoom link?
The default subject line is **[Meeting Topic] Confirmation.** This means the subject line will be what you called the meeting, followed by the word **Confirmation.** I recommend you change the word Confirmation to **ZOOM LINK.**

Any information you want your participants to have easily accessible as they join your event should be typed into the white box.

Branding

- Banner: Upload a horizontal image that will be displayed at the top of your registration page.

- Logo: Upload a square image that will appear to the right of the meeting topic on the registration page.

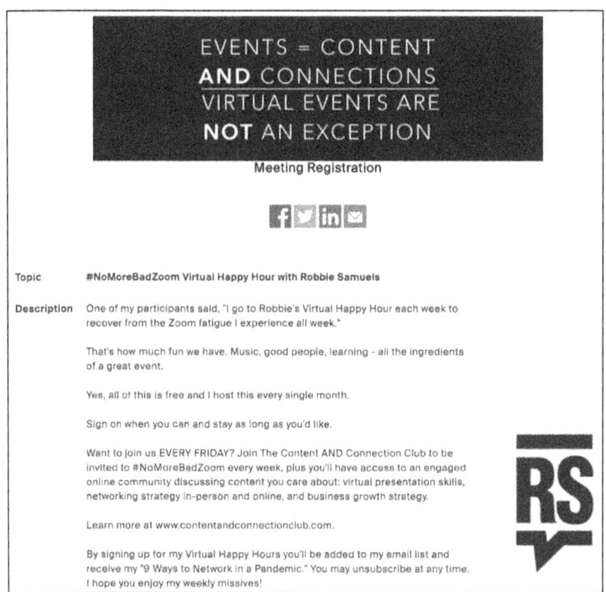

FIGURE 9.14. This branding example shows the #NoMoreBadZoom Virtual Happy Hour registration page - www.NoMoreBadZoom.com. Register to join us on the first Friday of each month!

Images not displaying correctly? Be sure you're following the suggested image requirements.

CAPTIONS, SIGN LANGUAGE INTERPRETATION, LANGUAGE INTERPRETATION

Free Live Captions Through Zoom

There are many reasons to be excited that Zoom provides free access to live captions and saves the transcription when you record your event.

- Ever wanted to capture the exact text for a script your coach provided but didn't want to have to watch the entire coaching call replay video to find that section?

- Would you like to make your event a bit more accessible to someone who is Deaf or hearing-impaired and would find it beneficial to read along as they listened?

If your main reason for using live captions is to create a more accessible event, I'm sorry to tell you that AI-generated captions are not going to be sufficient. Within the Deaf community, they are called "craptions," because a word or two being incorrect could change the entire meaning of the presentation. Nothing replaces quality sign language interpreters for creating an accessible event.

There are other reasons to enable this feature and use it for every meeting. I have turned it on and moved the captions to the top of my screen to help me decipher audio from someone with an accent that I'm not able to understand very well. It helped, although AI captions are often even less accurate if the speaker doesn't have a neutral American accent (think Johnny Carson and Stephen Colbert).[25]

Want to improve the quality of your captions on Zoom?
Otter.ai provides closed captions for Otter Pro and Otter Business users who have Zoom Pro or higher. Otter.ai lets you create a Custom Vocabulary so that proper names, jargon, acronyms, and unique name spellings are more accurately transcribed.[26]

I give my business growth strategy coaching clients the ability to record our sessions and download the full transcript.[27] Then, if they want to revisit something we discussed, they can search for keywords in the transcript to find the text and read that portion to view the AI-generated text. This saves them the time it takes to watch the entire session and gives them 80% or more of the text they need.

Save Transcript

When setting up live captions in **Zoom.us Settings**, there's an option to allow participants to save the transcript.[28] If that's been enabled, participants need to click **View Full Transcript** under the CC (a.k.a. close captioning) button when they join the meeting. If they click this option later in the meeting, it will only show the transcript from that point. If a participant has permission to record, the files will include the transcript from when they hit record.

Sign Language Interpretation

Zoom allows you to assign up to 20 sign language interpreters (however, they do not provide interpreters). This is a relatively new feature, released in late 2022. Rather than spotlighting the sign language interpreter next to the speaker, this new feature allows any participant to choose the sign language interpretation option to view a separate video which they may resize or relocate anywhere on their screen. Unfortunately, when using this feature, the sign language interpretation video *will not* be recorded if you're not viewing it on your screen—although the participant viewing the separate video may be able to record to their computer (however, I have not tested this).

This feature doesn't work with the Personal Meeting ID (PMI). It also needs to be selected when scheduling a meeting (it won't work for an instant meeting). To initiate and manage this feature, the host must join the meeting via the Zoom desktop client, not a mobile device or the web client.[29]

Language Interpretation

This allows you to assign a participant to translate simultaneously from one spoken language to another. If you don't see this option when setting up a meeting, enable it at **Zoom.us Settings**.[30] You can then select which language the interpreter will translate from and into. If you don't see the language you want listed, you can add it. Then, when you schedule a meeting, you can add language interpretation and assign specific participants as translators in advance or during the meeting. Doing so will display the language interpretation option in the meeting at the bottom of the Zoom window (the button icon is a globe). Participants click on the globe to view options and select a language audio channel.

To record the second language, give a participant listening to that language channel permission to record to their computer. This feature doesn't work with the Personal Meeting ID (PMI).[31]

Captions in another language
For $50 a year, participants can view automated captions in a language other than English. This is available in Zoom Meetings and Zoom Webinars. [32]

You did it! If you're reading this, you've found and updated all the settings you'll need to create an amazing virtual experience. You now have all the ingredients and cooking equipment you need, but you may need a basic recipe to get started before you can truly make use of these features. That's what I cover in the rest of this book. Use the table of contents to decide where to go next, or I recommend reading from Chapter Two, *Getting Set Up for Success,* so you look and sound good while creating a transformative, inclusive, and engaging virtual event.

Conclusion

When I first launched The 5% Advantage Program in April 2020 to help speakers and meeting professionals become more confident and competent using Zoom, my wife incredulously said, "Who wants to get just 5% better?!?"

I explained that the goal is to become 5% better *every time* you Zoom. Think about how amazing you would be if you had that kind of consistent improvement.

This book is filled with strategies to help you get 5% better the next time you Zoom. Take a moment and jot down a few strategies you plan to use.

Perhaps it is. . .

- Closing the waiting room once you're ready to start your meeting.
- Using the on-deck method to give participants a heads-up that you're about to call on them.
- Telling participants in what order they should speak in breakout rooms.

Individually, these are all simple strategies. As you get used to doing one, you add another, and then another, until your virtual sessions are distinctly better than they are now.

Virtual facilitation skills, like those mentioned above, were just one of two consistent themes in this book that are not tied specifically to using the Zoom platform. The other is purpose-first design. Taking time before your meeting to think about the transformation your participants will have because of your meeting will help you design with those objectives in mind.

If you consistently try to improve your skills as a virtual presenter and virtual facilitator, and you regularly apply purpose-first design, you will become sought after—not just for your content—but also for the experience you create online.

I recommend that you download all the checklists, step-by-step guides, and videos mentioned throughout the book. You can do that at www. robbiesamuels.com/breakout.

Remember, you don't have to do this alone.

I offer a variety of services, including coaching and training, to help you create transformative, inclusive, and engaging virtual sessions. Everything from a one-hour consult to share my ideas for your event design, to training your team and speakers, to producing your multi-day virtual conference.

Let me and my team reduce the stress for you and your team.

Flip back to the opening pages of this book, and you'll see testimonials from clients and speakers I've supported, as they shifted their virtual programs away from death-by-PowerPoint to a vibrant community activity.

I'd be honored to help you do the same. Visit www.robbiesamuels. com/virtual-event-design to find out how I support my event clients.

Finally, I'd love to hear from you! Let me know what you plan to do differently because of this book. Forward me compliments you receive from participants. Tell me how your speakers feel better prepared and more confident about their virtual presentations. And let me know what questions you still have unanswered, so I can address them in the future.

I can't wait to hear it all. Email action@BreakOutofBoredom.com to share your good news.

NOTES

**All links are available with the other resources at
www.robbiesamuels.com/breakout.**

INTRODUCTION

1 "Speaking." n.d. Robbie Samuels LLC. Accessed January 20, 2023.
http://www.robbiesamuels.com/ speaking.

2 "On the Schmooze." n.d. Robbie Samuels LLC. Accessed January 20, 2023.
http://www.OntheSchmooze. com.

3 "Croissants vs. Bagels." n.d. Robbie Samuels LLC. Accessed January 20, 2023.
http://www. CroissantsvsBagels.com.

4 "Hate networking? Stop bageling and be the croissant!" YouTube. January 22,
2020. http://www.robbiesamuels.com/TEDx.

5 "Why Business School is a Great Time to Network." Harvard Business Review.
April 15, 2019. https://hbr.org/2019/04/why-business-school-is-a-great-time-
to-network.

6 "#NoMoreBadZoom Virtual Happy Hour" n.d. Robbie Samuels LLC. Accessed
January 20, 2023. http:// www.NoMoreBadZoom.com.

7 "The 5% Advantage Program." n.d. Robbie Samuels LLC. Accessed January 20,
2023. http://www. the5percentadvantage.com.

8 "Small List, Big Results." n.d. Robbie Samuels LLC. Accessed January 20, 2023.
http://www. SmallListBigResults.com.

9 Bejan, Bob. "8 Ways to Rethink Virtual Events for the Age of Social
Distancing." Fast Company. May 4, 2020. https://www.fastcompany.
com/90499636/8-ways-to-rethink-virtual-events-for-the-age-of-social-
distancing.

CHAPTER ONE

1 "The People's Gathering." n.d. Pacific Lutheran University. Accessed January
22, 2023. https://www.plu.edu/continuing-education/diversity-equity-and-
inclusion/the-peoples-gathering/.

2 "Homepage." n.d. California WIC Association. Accessed January 22, 2023.
https://www.calwic.org.

3 "Homepage." n.d. Conveners.org. Accessed January 22, 2023.
https://conveners.org/.

4 "Meetings and webinars comparison." Zoom. October 6, 2022. https://support.zoom.us/hc/en-us/articles/115005474943-Meetings-and-webinars-comparison.

5 Ibid.

6 Ibid.

7 "Why Join NSA?." n.d. National Speakers Association. Accessed January 22, 2023. https://nsaspeaker.org/join.

CHAPTER TWO

1 Download the #NoMoreBadZoom Settings Checklist and other resources at http://www.robbiesamuels.com/breakout.

2 "Homepage." n.d. Elisabeth Steele LLC. Accessed January 20, 2023 https://www.elisabethsteele.com.

3 "Bekada LED Desk Light with Clamp." n.d. Amazon. Accessed January 22, 2023. https://amzn.to/3kDGdcU. (Affiliate link.)

4 "The Real Reason Home Improvement Always Hid Wilson's Face." Screenrant. July 24, 2022. https://screenrant.com/home-improvement-show-wilson-face-hidden-tim-allen-memory.

5 "Is there any psychological benefit to the superman pose?" Open Access Government. May 16, 2022. https://www.openaccessgovernment.org/superman-pose-power-posing-confidence-boost/135719/#.

6 "Virtual Backgrounds." n.d. Zoom App Marketplace. Accessed January 22, 2023. https://marketplace.zoom.us/apps/bds99mN4S_i7ktJINgsNXw.

7 "Zoom Virtual Background system requirements." Zoom. December 6, 2022. https://support.zoom.us/hc/en-us/articles/360043484511-Zoom-Virtual-Background-system-requirements.

8 "Using blurred background." Zoom. September 26, 2022. https://support.zoom.us/hc/en-us/articles/360061468611-Using-blurred-background-.

9 "The Wood With a Story to Tell." Siberian Heritage store. n.d. Amazon. Accessed January 22, 2023. https://amzn.to/3wFx3iR. (Affiliate link.)

10 "Upgrade Your Video Experience." Logitech store. n.d. Amazon. Accessed January 20, 2023. https://amzn.to/3QtYyEY. (Affiliate link.)

11 "PlexiCam: Makes great eye-contact online easy." n.d. PlexiCam. Accessed January 20, 2023. https://www.plexicam.com.

12 "Camo." n.d. Reincubate. Accessed January 20, 2023. https://reincubate.com/camo.

13 Search results for "flexible phone tripod." n.d. Amazon. Accessed January 22, 2023. https://amzn.to/3kDjePa. (Affiliate link.)

14 Gouhari, Yasmin. "Poor Audio Causes our Brains to Work 35% Harder to Interpret Information, EPOS Study Finds." EPOS. November 2, 2022. https://www.eposaudio.com/en/us/contact/pressroom/press-releases/poor-audio-causes-our-brains-to-work-35-harder-to-interpret-information-epos-study-finds#.

15 Gersema, Emily. "Audio Quality Influences Whether You Believe What You Hear." USC Dornsife College. University of Southern California. April 23, 2018. https://dornsife.usc.edu/news/stories/2792/audio-quality-influences-whether-you-believe-what-you-hear/.

16 "Professional Home Studio Set-up." Robbie Samuels LLC. December 13, 2022. https://robbiesamuels.com/professional-home-studio-podcast-set-up/.

17 "Shure SM7B." n.d. Amazon. Accessed January 20, 2023. https://amzn.to/3Qu3UQA. (Affiliate link.)

18 "Shure MV7." n.d. Amazon. Accessed January 20, 2023. https://amzn.to/3Gx6gJM. (Affiliate link.)

19 "Blue Yeti." n.d. Amazon. Accessed January 20, 2023. https://amzn.to/3CEfUcF. (Affiliate link.)

20 "Speak with Confidence in Business Calls." n.d. Krisp. Accessed January 20, 2023. https://krisp.ai/.

CHAPTER THREE

1 "Setting a custom gallery view." Zoom. June 1, 2022. https://support.zoom.us/hc/en-us/articles/4413866054285-Setting-a-custom-gallery-view-order-.

2 "Meeting Settings." n.d. Zoom. Accessed January 20, 2023. https://zoom.us/profile/setting.

3 Ibid.

4 Ibid.

5 "HIPAA Business Associate Agreement (BAA)." Zoom. October 6, 2022. https://support.zoom.us/hc/en-us/articles/207652183-HIPAA-Business-Associate-Agreement-BAA-.

6 "Meeting Settings." Zoom.

7 Ibid.

CHAPTER FOUR

1 "Enjoy Cinematic Presentations with Canva." n.d. Canva. Accessed January 20, 2023. https://www.canva.com/presentations/.

2 "Homepage." n.d. Donna Mack, Disability Diplomat. Accessed January 20, 2023. https://disabilitydiplomat.com/.

3 "Homepage." n.d. Nicolas Steenhout, disability consultant. Accessed January 20, 2023. https://incl.ca.

CHAPTER FIVE

1 "HomeDadCon." n.d. The National At-Home Dad Network. Accessed January 20, 2023. https://athomedad.org/homedadcon/.

2 "Homepage." n.d. Notary Symposium. Accessed January 20, 2023. http://www.notarysymposium.com.

3 "Homepage." n.d. Get Known Strategy. Accessed January 24, 2023. https://www.getknownstrategy.com/.

4 "Homepage." n.d. Sensible Woo. Accessed January 24, 2023. https://sensiblewoo.com/.

5 "How to create Uber vouchers." n.d. Uber. Accessed January 24, 2023. https://www.uber.com/blog/how-to-create-uber-vouchers/.

6 "Customizing meeting email templates." Zoom. August 18, 2022. https://support.zoom.us/hc/en-us/articles/360061260912-Customizing-meeting-email-templates.

7 "Customized webinar email templates and settings." Zoom. September 7, 2022. https://support.zoom.us/hc/en-us/articles/203686335-Customizing-webinar-email-templates-and-settings.

8 "#NoMoreBadZoom Virtual Happy Hour." Robbie Samuels.

9 "Happy Child stock photo - credit Studio1One." n.d. iStock by Getty Images. Accessed January 24, 2023. https://www.istockphoto.com/photo/happy-child-gm146746272-8350306.

10 "CloudValley Webcam Cover Slide [2-Pack]." n.d. Amazon. Accessed January 24, 2023. https://amzn.to/3JdAaFW. (Affiliate link.)

11 "Create an on-screen timer." n.d. Microsoft. Accessed January 24, 2023. https://support.microsoft.com/en-us/office/create-an-on-screen-timer-4c3a70d3-8d59-4972-a368-8b4ffc31a606.

12 "Slides Timer." n.d. Chrome Web Store. Accessed January 24, 2023. https://chrome.google.com/webstore/detail/slides-timer/nfhjdkmpebifdelclimjfaackjhiglpc?hl=en.

13 "PowerPoint presentations in a window not full screen." Office Watch. July 28, 2022. https://office-watch.com/2022/powerpoint-presentations-in-window-not-full-screen/#.

14 "Enabling polling for meetings." Zoom.us January 13, 2023. https://support.zoom.us/hc/en-us/articles/4412324684685-Enabling-polling-for-meetings.

15 Ibid.

16 "What is your ZoomScore™?" n.d. Rosemary Ravinal. Accessed January 25, 2023. http://rosemaryravinal.com/resources/#zoomscore.

17 "Creating breakout rooms from poll results." Zoom. January 16, 2023. https://support.zoom.us/hc/en-us/articles/12211651297933.

18 "Conducting advanced polls and quizzes in meetings." Zoom. December 21, 2022. https://support.zoom.us/hc/en-us/articles/4412325214477.

19 "Using non-verbal feedback and meeting reactions." Zoom. January 4, 2023. https://support.zoom.us/hc/en-us/articles/115001286183-Using-non-verbal-feedback-and-meeting-reactions-.

20 "Using annotation tools for collaboration." Zoom. December 9, 2022. https://support.zoom.us/hc/en-us/articles/115005706806-Using-annotation-tools-for-collaboration.

21 "Getting started with Zoom Apps." Zoom. January 23, 2023. https://support.zoom.us/hc/en-us/articles/360061554732-Getting-started-with-Zoom-Apps-.

22 "Discover apps." n.d. Zoom. Accessed January 25, 2023. https://marketplace.zoom.us/.

23 "Phone tripod search results." n.d. Amazon. Accessed January 20, 2023. https://amzn.to/3wel8by. (Affiliate link.)

24 "Sharing your iOS screen from the Zoom desktop client." Zoom. May 23, 2022. https://support.zoom.us/hc/en-us/articles/201379235-Sharing-your-iOS-screen-from-the-Zoom-desktop-client.

25 "Small List, Big Results." n.d. Robbie Samuels LLC.

26 "Getting started with Zoom reporting." Zoom. January 11, 2023. https://7support.zoom.us/hc/en-us/articles/201363213-Getting-started-with-Zoom-reporting.

27 "Minthouz Cube Timer." n.d. Amazon. Accessed January 25, 2023. https://www.amazon.com/Minthouz-Kitchen-Management-Countdown-Settings/dp/B095WJJNFM/ref=sr_1_8?keywords=cube+timer&qid=1674149002&sr=8-8.

CHAPTER SIX

1 "Managing breakout rooms." Zoom. December 27, 2022. https://support.zoom.us/hc/en-us/articles/206476313.

2 "Managing breakout rooms." Zoom. January 26, 2023. https://support.zoom.us/hc/en-us/articles/206476313-Managing-breakout-rooms.

3 "Zoom Software Quarterly Lifecycle Policy." Zoom. January 19, 2023. https://support.zoom.us/hc/en-us/articles/360059429231-Zoom-Software-Quarterly-Lifecycle-Policy.

4 "Enabling breakout rooms." Zoom. January 20, 2023. https://support.zoom.us/hc/en-us/articles/206476093-Enabling-breakout-rooms.

5 "Creating breakout rooms from poll results." Zoom. January 16, 2023. https://support.zoom.us/hc/en-us/articles/12211651297933.

6 Ibid.

7 "Ask Deep Questions." n.d. Jan Keck. Accessed January 20, 2023. http://www.askdeepquestions.com/.

8 "Climer Cards." n.d. Climer Cards. Accessed January 20, 2023. https://climercards.com.

9 "#NoMoreBadZoom Virtual Happy Hour." Robbie Samuels.

10 "Sharing screen and broadcasting to breakout rooms." Zoom. December 20, 2022. https://support.zoom.us/hc/en-us/articles/8550395207693-Sharing-screen-and-broadcasting-to-breakout-rooms.

11 Ibid.

12 "Side-by-side mode for screen sharing." Zoom. October 17, 2022. https://support.zoom.us/hc/en-us/articles/115004802843-Side-by-side-mode-for-screen-sharing.

13 "Managing participants in a meeting." Zoom. December 20, 2022. https://support.zoom.us/hc/en-us/articles/115005759423-Managing-participants-in-a-meeting.

CHAPTER EIGHT

1 "How to Keep Uninvited Guests Out of Your Zoom Meeting." Zoom. July 26, 2021. https://blog.zoom.us/keep-uninvited-guests-out-of-your-zoom-meeting.

2 "Meeting Settings." Zoom.

3 "Using Waiting Room." Zoom.us. December 20, 2022. https://support.zoom.us/hc/en-us/articles/115000332726-Using-Waiting-Room.

4 "Muting all participants when they join a meeting." Zoom.us. December 15, 2021. https://support.zoom.us/hc/en-us/articles/360060860512-Muting-all-participants-when-they-join-a-meeting.

5 "Enabling the new meeting chat experience." Zoom.us. January 13, 2023. https://support.zoom.us/hc/en-us/articles/11402067412109-Enabling-the-new-meeting-chat-experience.

6 "Enabling screen sharing for participants in Zoom meetings." Zoom.us November 22, 2022. https://support.zoom.us/hc/en-us/articles/9488811744909-Enabling-screen-sharing-for-participants-in-Zoom-meetings.

7 "Enabling or disabling annotation tools for meetings." Zoom.us. December 10, 2021. https://support.zoom.us/hc/en-us/articles/4409894568845-Enabling-or-disabling-annotation-tools-for-meetings.

8 "Sharing your screen or desktop on Zoom." Zoom.us. November 4, 2022. https://support.zoom.us/hc/en-us/articles/201362153-Sharing-your-screen-or-desktop-on-Zoom.

9 "Allowing participants/panelists to rejoin." Zoom.us October 6, 2022. https://support.zoom.us/hc/en-us/articles/360021851371-Allowing-participants-panelists-to-rejoin.

10 "#NoMoreBadZoom Virtual Happy Hour." Robbie Samuels.

11 "Reporting inappropriate behavior." Zoom. November 28, 2022. https://support.zoom.us/hc/en-us/articles/360042791091-Reporting-inappropriate-behavior.

12 Ibid.

13 "In-meeting security." Zoom. November 30, 2022. https://support.zoom.us/hc/en-us/articles/360041848151-In-meeting-security-options.

CHAPTER NINE

1 "Meeting Settings." Zoom.

2 "Profile Settings." n.d. Zoom. Accessed January 20, 2023. https://us06web.zoom.us/profile/setting.

3 "Changing Settings in the Desktop Client/Mobile App." Zoom. January 18, 2023. https://support.zoom.us/hc/en-us/articles/201362623-Changing-settings-in-the-desktop-client-mobile-app.

4 "Plans & Pricing." n.d. Zoom. Accessed January 20, 2023. https://zoom.us/pricing.

5 "Changing Your Name on Zoom." Zoom. August 26, 2022. https://support.zoom.us/hc/en-us/articles/8715431556621-Changing-your-name-on-Zoom.

6 "Profile Settings." n.d. Zoom.

7 "Starting the Zoom desktop client." Zoom. September 28, 2022. https://support.zoom.us/hc/en-us/articles/360032812931-Starting-the-Zoom-desktop-client.

8 "Automatic update release frequencies." Zoom. September 6, 2022. https://support.zoom.us/hc/en-us/articles/4413422750861.

9 "Adjusting your video layout during a virtual meeting." Zoom. September 26, 2022. https://support.zoom.us/hc/en-us/articles/201362323-Adjusting-your-video-layout-during-a-virtual-meeting.

10 "OBS Project." OBS. Accessed January 20, 2023. https://obsproject.com.

11 "Meet Ecamm Live." Ecamm. Accessed January 20, 2023. https://www.ecamm.com.

12 "Meeting Settings." Zoom.

13 Sandra Fauconnier, CC BY-SA 4.0 <https://creativecommons.org/licenses/by-sa/4.0>, via Wikimedia Commons.

14 "Cloud recording storage capacity." Zoom. October 27, 2022. https://support.zoom.us/hc/en-us/articles/360060661511-Cloud-recording-storage-capacity.

15 "Managing and sharing cloud recordings." Zoom. January 20, 2023. https://support.zoom.us/hc/en-us/articles/205347605-Managing-and-sharing-cloud-recordings#.

16 "Plans & Pricing." Zoom.

17 "Modifying recording notification prompts." Zoom. October 14, 2022. https://support.zoom.us/hc/en-us/articles/360000486746-Modifying-recording-notification-prompts#.

18 "Automatic update release frequencies." Zoom. September 6, 2022. https://support.zoom.us/hc/en-us/articles/4413422750861.

19 "Zoom Software Quarterly Lifecycle Policy." Zoom.

20 "Uninstall apps on your Mac." n.d. Apple. Accessed January 20, 2023. https://support.apple.com/en-us/HT202235.

21 "Uninstall or remove apps and programs in Windows." n.d. Microsoft. Accessed January 20, 2023. https://support.microsoft.com/en-us/windows/uninstall-or-remove-apps-and-programs-in-windows-4b55f974-2cc6-2d2b-d092-5905080eaf98.

22 "Meeting Settings." Zoom.

23 Ibid.

24 Ibid.

25 "Is There a Place in America Where People Speak with Neutral Accents?" Atlas Obscura. August 23, 2016. https://www.atlasobscura.com/articles/neutral-american-accent#.

26 "Zoom Captions." n.d. Otter.ai. Accessed January 20, 2023. https://otter.ai/blog/zoom-captions.

27 Coaching & Mastermind." n.d. Robbie Samuels LLC. Accessed January 24, 2023. http://www.robbiesamuels.com/coaching-mastermind.

28 "Meeting Settings." Zoom.

29 "Using sign language interpretation in a meeting or webinar." Zoom. December 21, 2022. https://support.zoom.us/hc/en-us/articles/9644962487309-Using-sign-language-interpretation-in-a-meeting-or-webinar.

30 "Meeting Settings." Zoom.

31 "Using Language Interpretation in your meeting or webinar." Zoom. January 21, 2023. https://support.zoom.us/hc/en-us/articles/360034919791-Using-Language-Interpretation-in-your-meeting-or-webinar.

32 "Plans & Pricing." Zoom.

ACKNOWLEDGMENTS

I did not plan to write a third book so soon after releasing my second book in October 2021. Soon after that book was launched, a publisher contacted me about writing a book about Zoom. It wasn't a good fit, as they wanted the focus to be on workplaces, not conference presentations, but it got me thinking about the possibility. My first thanks to that publisher for getting the wheels turning. My long-time virtual assistant, Peya Robbins, strongly encouraged me to make this a reality, pointing out that I'd already created tons of content on this subject. Peya, thank you for the push and for keeping my business running while I focused on this project.

None of this would have come to pass if my first forays into virtual events were not well-received. For that, I have to thank the participants who showed up for my first virtual happy hour on March 13, 2020, and, even more so, the regular attendees of my #NoMoreBadZoom Virtual Happy Hour who showed up weekly all through 2020—even on Christmas and New Year's Eve!

It was amazing to see Amber Browning-Coyle, Annette Mason, Annie Hopson, Bil Lewis, Carol Mills, David Fox, Dorothy Wilhelm, DurgaMata Chaudhuri, Erika Salloux, Gayle Lantz, Ian Magrisso, Jen Bonardi, JM Evans, Jodi Pavia, Julia Goldstein, Kathleen Graffunder, Kristine Ace, Lisa Goldstein, Lynne Williams, Mee-Thlen Moy, Nancy Zare, Patricia Gaffney, Rachel Wagner, Reef Karim, Regina Carey, Robert Butwin, Sophie Lechner, Stefanie Kessen, and 20 to 30 other participants every Friday throughout 2020. Several have stepped up to help me co-host this event as our numbers grew, and it quickly became unwieldy to host on my own. Some of these regulars are still attending regularly to this day—three years later!

Generous experts shared their knowledge with our #NoMoreBadZoom Virtual Happy Hour community, so we could all keep getting better at leveraging virtual tools: Amy Climer, Amy Forrester, Bil Lewis, Brian Fanzo, Caitlin Krause, Charlene DeCesare, Charlene Tessier, Chris Scavongelli & Ilsa Webeck, Christopher G. Johnson, Crystal Washington, Dan Keldsen, Deb Reuben, Dorothy Wilhelm, Elisabeth Steele, Emily Merrell, Iggy Perillo, Jan Keck, Jean Marie DiGiovanna, Jen Bonardi, Jenny Ro, Julia Phelan, Kate Bays, Lisa Rothman, Luis Serrano, Dr. Margarita Gurri & Marilyn Suttle, Marie Incontrera, Mary Williams, Megan Amundson, Nicole Ouellette, Rob Ferre, Rosemary Ravinal, Shannan Slevin, Tami Evans, Terrell Jones, Tom Briggs, and Warwick Merry.

I was not thinking about creating a global networking event when I selected 5 p.m. ET as the event start time for that first virtual happy hour. But that's what happened. I'm so appreciative to the participants who joined very late or very early from Afghanistan, Albania, Argentina, Australia, Bermuda, Bosnia, Brunei, Canada, China, Colombia, Costa Rica, Czech Republic, Egypt, France, Germany, Honduras, Hong Kong, India, Indonesia, Iraq, Ireland, Jamaica, Japan, Kuwait, Malaysia, Mexico, Mongolia, The Netherlands, New Zealand, Palestinian Territories, Panama, Philippines, Romania, Russia, Slovenia, South Africa, Spain, Switzerland, Trinidad and Tobago, Turkey, Ukraine, and the United Kingdom.

I'm grateful to the pilot participants of The 5% Advantage Program, who committed to attend a May 2020 four-week program to become more confident and competent using Zoom: Annette Mason, Carol Mills, Charlene Tessier, Gina Warner, Julia Gessner, Lisa Goldstein, Lynn Festa, Megan Amundson, Michaela Wladasch, Nicole Ouellette, Peya Robbins, Rebecca Zucker, Simonia Blassingame, and Susan Kuepfer.

Their trust meant I could pour my energy into turning the pilot into a certification program, which happened a couple of months later.

Sixteen students earned the Certified Virtual Event Professional #No-MoreBadZoom designation: Alakesha Murray-Razzaqel, Charlene Tessier, Christopher G. Johnson, David Fox, Dorita Hatchett, Dorothy Wilhelm, Gayle Lantz, James Boggie, Jen Bonardi, Jeorgia' Brown, Jodi Pavia, Dr. Margarita Gurri, Marilyn Suttle, Rachel Wagner, Rocky Williams, and Simonia Blassingame.

I'm incredibly honored that in 2020, several organizations asked me to support their virtual events, allowing me to apply the event design strategies I had been experimenting with through my weekly virtual happy hour. Huge thanks to the Association for Talent Development (ATD) Southern Connecticut Chapter, BNI Commerce Connection, California Breastfeeding Coalition, California WIC Association, Coatesville Youth Initiative, Feeding America, Iowa 80 Group, National At-Home Dad Network, Notary Symposium, Success thru Style, U.S. Embassy in Mexico, ValleyCare Charitable Foundation, and VNS Health.

An additional shout-out to my team of Zoom producers, who have helped support my event clients over the last three years and given me the "bench strength" to develop a sustainable business: Christopher G. Johnson, Jen Bonardi, Nicole Ouellette, and Peya Robbins.

My world would be incomplete without my wife, Jess Samuels. She married me knowing I was entrepreneurial and believed I could create a successful business. With her unyielding support, ten years later, I finally became an "overnight success." She stuck with me through all the many twists and turns that the pandemic threw at my in-person events-focused business. Planning for our children's future was the fuel that kept me going throughout the endless days of 2020.

ABOUT THE AUTHOR

Robbie Samuels is an event design consultant and executive Zoom producer who is recognized as a networking expert by NPR, PCMA, Harvard Business Review, Forbes, Lifehacker, and Inc. He has also been recognized as an expert in virtual event design by JDC Events, and is a Certified Virtual Convener and Certified Virtual Presenter. His event clients are national and statewide advocacy organizations, including Feeding America and California WIC Association.

He is the author of three books, *Break Out of Boredom: Low-Tech Solutions for Highly Engaging Zoom Events*, *Small List, Big Results: Launch a Successful Offer No Matter the Size of Your Email List*, and *Croissants vs. Bagels: Strategic, Effective, and Inclusive Networking at Conferences.*

Robbie is a professional speaker, TEDx speaker, and a *Harvard Business Review* contributor, who has been featured in numerous leading business publications and business books. Since 2016, he's hosted the *On the Schmooze* podcast and, since 2020, #NoMoreBadZoom Virtual Happy Hours.

He is the out transgender owner of Robbie Samuels LLC, a certified LGBT Business Enterprise. Robbie resides in the Philadelphia area with his wife and two children. Learn more about him and his work at www.robbiesamuels.com.

A REQUEST

THANK YOU
for Reading My Book!

I would love to hear from you. Writing a review (<u>www.robbiesamuels.com/BreakOutReview</u>) is as easy as answering any of these questions:

- What is your most valuable takeaway or insight?

- What have you done differently—or what will you do differently—because of what you read?

- Who would benefit from reading this book?

Seriously, just two or three sentences would be amazing. Your feedback helps to get this book into the hands of those who need it most.

I look forward to hearing about the action you took because of this book.

Thank you in advance,

Robbie

Download Free
Bonus Resources

READ THIS

To help you implement the strategies in this book, I've created several resources, including checklists, step-by-step guides, and 30+ videos. Download them all at no cost whatsoever. It's my gift to you. – Robbie Samuels

Go to www.robbiesamuels.com/breakout to get it!